Arnold Grummer's

COMPLETE GUIDE TO

Easy Papermaking

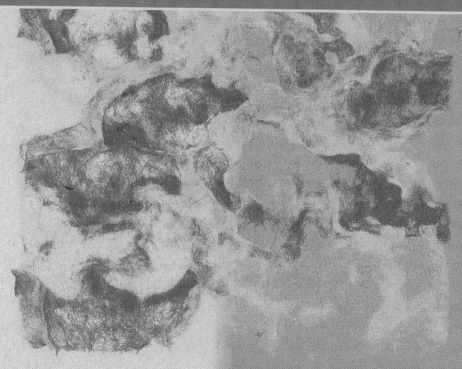

Published by

krause publications
An F&W Publications Company

700 East State Street • Iola, WI 54990-0001
715-445-2214 • 888-457-2873

Please call or write for our free catalog of publications. Our toll-free number to place an order or obtain a free catalog is (800) 258-0929 or please use our regular business telephone (715) 445-2214 for editorial comment and further information.

Cover design by Jon Stein
Book design by Jan Wojtech

Photography Credits
All photo and electronmicrographs in Chapters 3, 4, and 5: Microscopy Laboratories of the former Institute of Paper Chemistry (now the Institute of Paper Science and Technology).
Black and white photos in the Introduction: Fred Sweeney, head of the Photographic Laboratories of the Institute of Paper Chemistry.
Color setup photos: Don Ackerman Photography, New Berlin, Wis.
Color flat work: Pro Visual Photography, West Allis, Wis.; the author.

Art Credits
All paper sheets, shapes, forms, and castings by the author unless otherwise credited.
All color in this book's paper pieces is colored fibers—no paint.

Manufactured in the United States of America

Library of Congress Cataloging-in-Publication Data

Grummer, Arnold
        Arnold Grummer's Complete Guide to Easy Papermaking

ISBN 0-87341-710-0

1. Papermaking   2. Grummer   3. Title

                        98-86905
                        CIP

DEDICATION

To all my favorite people: Mabe, Mark, Ellen, Ed and Bill; Greg, Janet and Jack; Kim, Dave, Jon, Dan and Ellie; and any who yet may come.

ACKNOWLEDGMENTS

For this book's amazing and educational photo and electron micrographs and their meaning, I thank former Institute of Paper Chemistry electron microscopists, the late Olga Smith, Hilka Kaustinen, and Dr. Russell Parham. Their colleague, Jack Hankey, prepared and shared paper cross sections. Hopefully, through this book, what they so willingly and patiently shared with me will be extended to many others.

The outstanding photography and print production of Fred Sweeney and his Institute photography staff chronicled occurrences in and about the Dard Hunter Paper Museum as well as the Institute's whole scientific and educational program. The entire Institute staff, scientific and informational, has a direct connection with this book, because from them came all the background information from which its contents have sprung. Specialized watermark technology came from my Institute colleague and frequent co-lecturer, Bill (William C.) Krueger. Three extended interviews, granted by Institute colleagues late in my career there, are major to this book. Their sources are Dr. John Swanson, surface chemistry; Dr. Irwin A. Pearl, lignin; Dr. Dean Einspahr, forest genetics.

Fascinating paper insight came from the IPC 1478 Filter Paper research headed by Dr. J.A. Van Den Akker and Dr. Roy C. Whitney. I thank Dr. Bill Bliesner (Institute alumnus) of Filter Materials Corp. for discussion of paper pH matters.

Translating the above into this book relied repeatedly on encouragement from Kim Schiedermayer, my daughter, and more general support from my son Greg and my wife Mabe, whose combined creativity and labor have translated ideas and concepts into performing products. Kim's husband, Dr. David Schiedermayer (also an author), helped extensively in sheet selection to illustrate each technique.

Finally, I acknowledge support provided by a continuance of interest, encouragement, and positive response from thousands of people at trade shows, workshops, seminars, exhibits, and demonstrations over two decades. No writer is an island.

TABLE OF CONTENTS

Part I

Part II

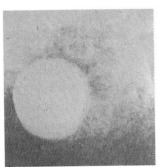

Part III

Part IV

PART

I

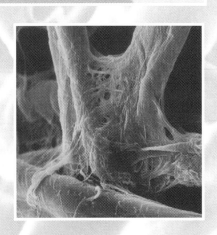

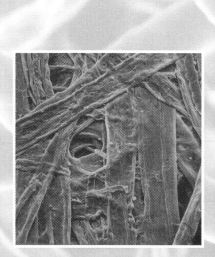

Introduction
Welcome to Arnold's World

This book pulls together much of what I have learned about paper and hand papermaking in 30 years of experimenting and pursuing the answer to "What if...." It reflects 16 years of experience with deep science and high technology accumulated at The Institute of Paper Chemistry in Appleton, Wisconsin; six years of in-depth historical immersion while curator of the Institute's Dard Hunter Paper Museum, and host to its visiting luminaries from most nooks of the earth; being cleared by the Federal Bureau of Investigation (FBI) for certain work and subsequently glimpsing, via my friend and Institute colleague Bill Krueger and his staff, areas of watermark-

(Above) Former President Richard M. Nixon holds the sheet of paper he made under the tutelage of Arnold Grummer (foreground, second from right) on the Great American Paper Machine.

(Right) Demonstrating hand papermaking on the historical streets of Galena, Ill.

ing and other exploration where likely no man had ever trod before. Heady stuff.

I watched patiently a three-year study on the development of a test for paper permanence. I followed with anticipation the development of callus in a petri dish and had the real joy of managing the press conference and introducing the scientists who developed the world's first test tube tree, which the callus eventually produced. I experienced real awe reading the final report on IPC 1478 Filter Paper which, courtesy of the first U2 "spy" planes, wrote the book on where radioactive debris entered, moved in, and left the atmosphere. On the basis of data delivered by the paper, atmospheric testing of radioactive devices was halted—certainly a stunning success for the Institute.

With mentoring from Dard Hunter, right, Arnold Grummer makes a sheet of paper with a hand mold from the collection of the Dard Hunter Paper Museum.

I read Ph.D. theses in about every science area touched by paper; debated environmental matters with steaming, over-emotional, irate college students; roamed verbally with Dard Hunter over homemade type, the pros and cons of Empress Shotoku and her million dharani, and the directional vagaries of Korean hand molds; edited and narrated a movie on Taiwan's handmade paper industry from footage taken by a former Kimberly-Clark executive; criss-crossed the Institute's laboratories with high school students, Japanese industrialists, and a variety of industry and general media. Some of this is cataloged in the publication I edited, *SCAN*. And this, of course, reflects only a few of the moments.

The momentum was so great that after leaving the Institute, I wrote about, demonstrated, talked and lectured on modern and historical papermaking all the way from the FBI Academy at Quantico, Virginia, and the Internal Revenue Service (IRS) in Chicago, to elementary schools in Arkansas, art festivals in Beaumont, Texas, to festivals and shows at the Smithsonian Institution in Washington, D.C. Also to the merry mix of science and people at the Museum of Science and Industry in Chicago and to a mix of art and printing audiences in Massachusetts (TAPPI), New York (SUNY College of Foresty, Syracuse), and Canada's London, Toronto, and Montreal.

Consequently, within this book lies a spread of information and range of do-able art and decorative techniques probably not matched in any other publication. But they are all quite visible in the more than 2,000 sheets scattered around my Quarter Moon Mill, made during my study and development of techniques. They constitute an invaluable reference.

And "do-able" is this publication's watchword. This book is largely hands-on and a hands-on book is no good if its projects cannot be carried out reasonably simply. Our criteria has been that if a technique could not be carried out by elementary school students, it would not appear in this book.

There has been much more in my paper world I would like to tell you about—sheets I have that are made of 11,000 and 30 million year-old fibers respectively, and the paper that survived 250 years underwater about a mile off Cape Kennedy and is today in almost pristine condition, the strange case of the "extraterrestrial" paper, and many of the amazing people paper thrust into my life or me into theirs—but if all of this is to be told, it will have to be in another book, because this introduction is too long already.

Happy papermaking. It's a pleasure to have you join me in my little corner of the world of paper.

A.E.G.

ABOUT THE BOOK
CHAPTER ONE

This book invites the general public, hobbyist, craftsperson and professional artist to a world of easy, no-experience, little-work hand papermaking that produces good, recognizable, and usable paper sheets immediately. Use of techniques in this book will result in paper as beautiful as it is immediate and easy.

The pour mold (page 36) used in most of these techniques provides for practically no work or time in preparation and cleanup. The pour mold can handle pulp in the sheet forming process so that anyone able to lift the mold out of water and hold it level while water drains, can make a near-perfect sheet the first time they try. Anyone. That is easy papermaking that is worthwhile.

But the dip mold (page 36) and its users are not excluded. The dip mold can accommodate all the techniques except those applied while pulp is in the deckle.

The artistic and decorative papermaking techniques presented are the primary purpose and motivation for this book. Because of the diversity and practical value of the techniques, this book will become a well-thumbed reference for every casual and serious papermaker interested in fiber manipulation for art and decoration.

Though it probably would not have been written were it not for the techniques, this book offers a broad array of other information, most of it in response to my interaction with people during 25 years of workshops, demonstrations, talks, the writing of two previous books, appearances on television, and six years as curator of the Dard Hunter Paper Museum.

The book begins by showing what kind of structure (paper) and building units (fibers) papermakers work with. With photo- and electron-micrographs created in the microscopy laboratories of the former Institute of Paper Chemistry, it likely surpasses in clarity and depth anything presented elsewhere.

The heavily visual section about paper is followed by the heavily hands-on section consisting of the basic hand papermaking steps and a variety of artistic and decorative projects. The function of the basic hand papermaking steps is twofold. First, they show how to make a plain sheet of paper. Second, some or all of the basic steps are part of the instructions for each project, and rather than repeating the information over and over, the instructions refer back to the basic steps used in that particular project.

This book does not cover Oriental papermaking. The length of the special bast fibers, the necessary forming aids and other additives, the special hand molds and their handling in sheet formation, make it a special field of work and study not within this book's intent. Mostly referred to as "Japanese papermaking," it can be seen in Timothy Barrett's comprehensive book listed in the bibliography. Also not covered are vacuum tables and fiber spray guns, both of which are simply exaggerations of things found in this book and which are rare even among well-equipped paper workshops and study centers.

For commercial papermaking kits and other equipment, the Appendix lists suppliers including Greg Markim, Inc., which specializes in the pour mold and manufactures my personally designed line of kits and equipment.

Now, on to that amazing engineering feat—paper.

GLOSSARY
CHAPTER TWO

It seems every vocation has a list of words with meanings specific to that endeavor. Papermaking is no exception. Read through this glossary and refer back to it if you run across an unfamiliar term while completing one of the projects.

Casting: Making a copy of a form or dimensional surface by applying wet pulp, then letting the pulp dry.

Couch: To remove a newly formed paper sheet (wet mat of fibers) from a papermaking screen. Too weak to be lifted off by hand, the new sheet is placed against a flat surface to which it will transfer when pressure is applied.

Couch Materials: Any materials with a surface that will cause a new sheet to transfer from a papermaking screen when the new sheet is pressed against it.

Couch Sheet: In papermaking, a reusable blotter sheet made especially for couching new sheets from papermaking screens.

Cover Screen: A piece of window screen or other suitable material laid over a newly formed paper sheet to protect the sheet during water removal with a sponge.

Curl and Cockle: The result of uneven shrinkage when a sheet of paper is not dried uniformly, such as when using an iron. Uneven drying means uneven shrinkage, pulling different parts of the sheet in different directions, causing either general curl or localized cockling, or both.

Deckle: The removable top part of a hand mold. The deckle sits on or fits around the papermaking screen and prevents pulp from running off the screen. Because it is the outer limits to which pulp can flow on the screen, the deckle determines the sheet's shape and size.

Dip Hand Mold: A hand mold which forms a sheet by being dipped into a vat full of pulp.

Drain Pan: Any tray, cookie pan, or similar container on which to lay a papermaking screen and newly formed sheet for initial water removal.

Drain Rack: Any grid-like structure placed in the drain pan upon which a screen and newly formed sheet can be placed to facilitate water drainage from the sheet. In some kits, the hand mold's screen support also serves as the drain rack.

Dry Lap: Dry pulp in sheet form.

Fiber: A fiber produced by a plant. It is cellulose and will bond naturally to other cellulose fibers when it touches them in water. Also sometimes used as a synonym for pulp.

Flock: A tendency of fibers to gather in bunches during sheet formation, instead of dispersing evenly as individuals. Flocking is visible when a sheet is held up to light.

Furnish: Pulp that consists of fibers plus all additives (sizing, opacifiers, fillers, etc.) required to make a specific type of paper.

Hand Mold: A device for making paper by hand. It consists of a screen, screen support, and a deckle.

Iron: In this book, an ordinary clothes iron used to quickly dry paper.

Ironing Board: A household ironing board or other fabric-covered surface where a damp sheet of paper can safely be ironed dry.

Pour Hand Mold: A hand mold that forms a sheet by having pulp poured into it.

Pulp: The raw material for making paper. It consists of individual fibers. Dry pulp is generally a sheet of fibers called "dry lap." Wet pulp is fibers in water. Papermakers generally begin with fibers in dry form.

Pulp Gun: Any container such as a turkey baster or mustard bottle used to dispense pulp by pressure.

Recycle: In this book, blending existing torn paper with water to disperse the fibers into wet pulp, then making the pulp into new paper.

Release Agent: A substance applied to a surface or form before wet pulp is applied in making a casting. When the pulp has dried, its removal from the surface or form is eased by the release agent.

Screen: Material woven or formed into a sieve-like fabric which will let water flow through but trap papermaking fibers on its surface. Previously, strands woven or laid side-by-side were primarily metal. Today, screens are primarily specially formulated plastic.

Slurry: In this book, water with fibers in it.

Vat: A container into which pulp is placed when a dip mold is used, and into which water is placed when a pour mold is used. The vat must be large enough to accommodate the hand mold and the papermaker's hands simultaneously.

Watermark: An image seen in paper when paper is held up to light.

WHAT PAPER IS

CHAPTER THREE

Paper is not a continuous substance like rolled-out pie dough or extruded plastic. It is a family of individual fibers living together in a sheet-shaped bundle. Each fiber has its own space but touches one or more other fibers. As discussed later, this is indeed a magic touch.

Individual fibers are brought to the bundle in water. When the fiber and water mixture is poured onto a screen, the water passes through the screen but the fiber doesn't. It is deposited on the bundle.

The first fibers of the bundle are deposited directly on the screen and succeeding fibers are deposited on top of them. This builds a series of layers which eventually become the sheet's thickness. These layers aid scientists in splitting the sheet the thin way when they want to explore the sheet's interior (for ink penetration, for example). You can probably do this yourself with a piece of transparent tape pressed on a paper surface and lifted up. Chances are one or more layers of fibers came up with the tape. Minus the layers, the sheet is thinner where the tape was applied. You can examine the sheet's interior at that point.

Fig. 3-1. *A magnified torn paper edge shows that paper is a mass of individual fibers. They are intertwined and, importantly, touching one another. The arrow points out a clearly defined single fiber.*

Fig. 3-2. We have said that paper is a batch of individual fibers. So if we magnify a sheet's surface, we should not see smoothness, but individual fibers. And indeed we do. Here is a magnified surface of a sheet. We see the fibers we write on, type on, or draw on. Also visible is the sheet's edge. It shows that the top layer of fibers is just one of many layers making up the entire sheet.

Two layers of the bundle are the outer (top and bottom) surfaces. Fibers in those layers can have a rough life. Sometimes, when assaulted with the unyielding metal of a ballpoint pen, surface fibers are dislodged and gather on the pen tip, making a mess of writing. Or tacky ink on a printing press might pull fibers loose, causing them to gather on a printing surface. Soon the printing is a mess.

The family bundle is happy to serve as it is or to put on a whole range of other persona by inviting into its midst chemicals, minerals, liquids, and solids. These might be sizings, opacifiers, brighteners, or fillers. The family bundle will also accept impregnation, saturation, lamination, or coating. Some of these completely encase the fiber family and the paper becomes merely a substrate.

The family's single-word motto is "versatility"—there are thousands of kinds of papers to meet thousands of different uses.

In this chapter, science's imaging technology has let us tour a batch of fibers making up a paper sheet. In the next chapter, let's visually tour a single fiber.

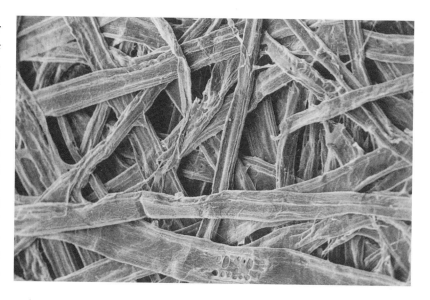

Fig. 3-3. *At even greater magnification, the sheet's surface fibers begin to take on specific physical personalities. Imagine the reaction as a pen's ballpoint rolls over the back of each fiber. For later reference, note a fiber at the bottom with an area of pitted surface.*

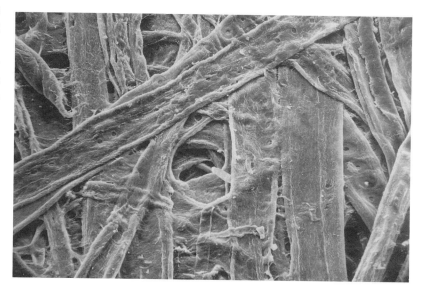

Fig. 3-4. *This even higher magnification opens up some interesting speculation. The fibers obviously do not touch each other all over. This leaves voids—openings between fibers on the sheet's surface. Made small enough, could a person crawl into the sheet through the opening seen here on the surface, continue down and around fibers where they don't touch, and finally come out on the other side? Very probably. It would be an interesting trip. So much for the family. Next, a tour of an individual fiber.*

WHAT A FIBER IS

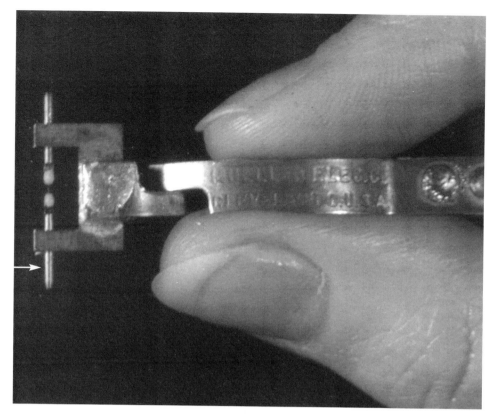

Fig. 4-1. This visual shows an individual papermaking fiber. It is mounted between the inside ends of two pins held vertically at the photo's far left (see arrow). The pins are held in upper and lower arms of a clamp held between a thumb and finger. Note the fiber's size in relation to the thumb and finger. Put your thumb over the thumb in the photo. That will show that the photo is somewhat enlarged. This fiber mount is special technology developed at the former Institute of Paper Chemistry for testing a fibers's tensile strength. It might be difficult or impossible to see the fiber in this photo, so see Fig. 4.2 below.

Fig. 4-2. This visual is a magnification of the two pin ends in the photo above. It shows that there really is a fiber, and gives us our first look at it. Also seen is the amazing technology developed at the former Institute of Paper Chemistry for gluing a fiber between two pin ends for a tensile strength test. Here, the fiber looks like a piece of string. But microscopy can tell much more. Look at the photos that follow.

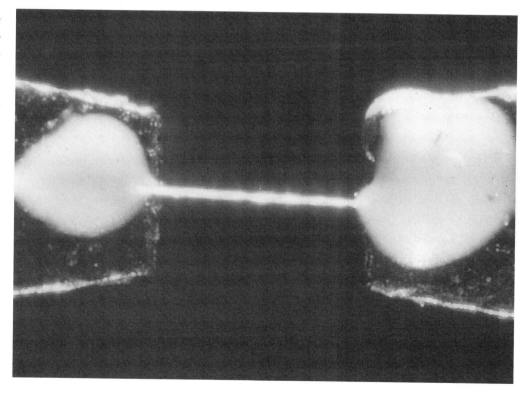

Fig. 4-3. *(Right) This higher magnification shows more. The fiber is generally round, somewhat irregular in diameter, and seemingly rough on the surface. Specifically, the surface is pitted, which takes us back to the photo on page 15. This fiber is wet and swollen as in its natural state. If the top were snipped off, we could look down and see that the fiber is hollow like a drinking straw. The hollow area is called the lumen. Note the surface pits.*

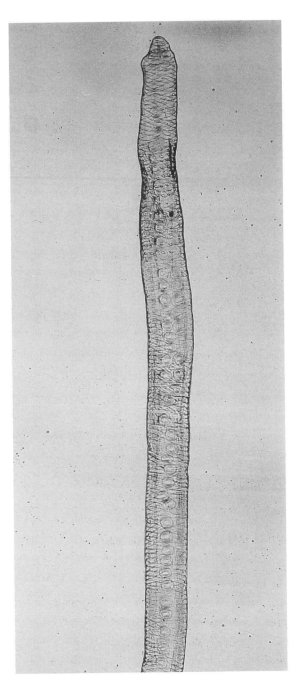

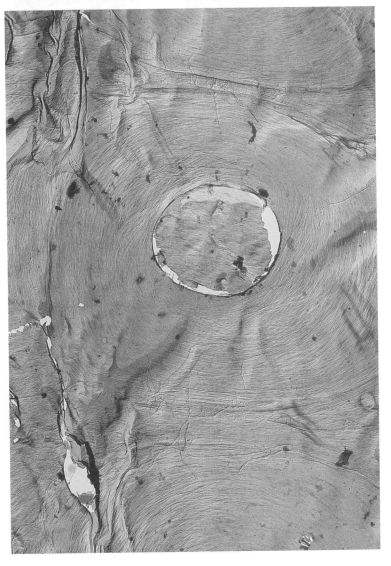

Fig. 4-4. *(Left) This is one of the many pits seen in Fig. 4-3. This original electronmicrograph was 20,000X magnification. It shows the extreme depth to which scientists have studied the papermaking fiber, and the amazing scientific instruments they have available. Actually, this pit is a food artery to the fiber's interior cells. This kind of revelation shows that common paper is hardly common, and might be one huge art gallery.*

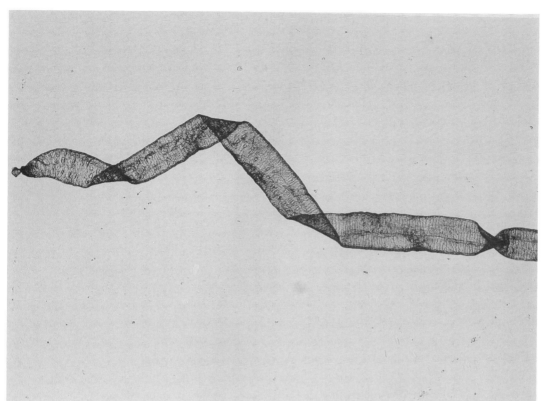

Fig. 4-5. *This is the wet swollen fiber seen in Fig. 4-4. When wet, the fiber's center is hollow. It's no surprise then, that when dried the fiber can collapse to look like a ribbon. Most fibers in most paper probably look like this, but see the next photo.*

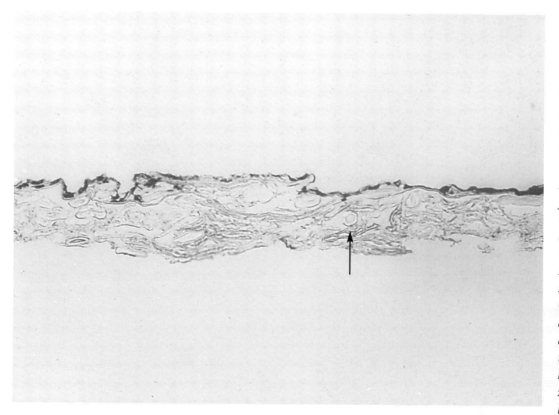

Fig. 4-6. *This cross section (cut edge) of a paper sheet is another view of fiber layers and of space between fibers. A fiber in the middle on the right shows a hollow center (see arrow). Apparently not all fibers collapse, which can affect sheet characteristics. Part of an ink penetration study, this cross section is of a Chicago telephone directory page. The dark section along the top is ink. For our last tour stop, let's zero in on the uncollapsed fiber showing its hollow center.*

Fig. 4-7. Imagine we have shrunk and stepped into the fiber's hollow center. Were we to scratch the fiber's wall around us, we might see this visual. It tells us the tiny papermaking fiber is itself made up of layers of tinier fibers, called fibrils. Several layers can be seen. Scientists likely don't know how many layers there might be. This electronmicrograph was made during that type of study. The original electron-micrograph was 40,000 times magnification. That provides some idea of the size of fibrils. (The fibril make-up of a fiber is of exceeding importance to paper. Read more about it in the following chapter.)

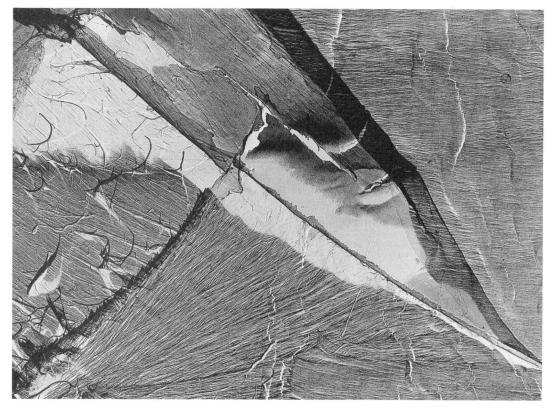

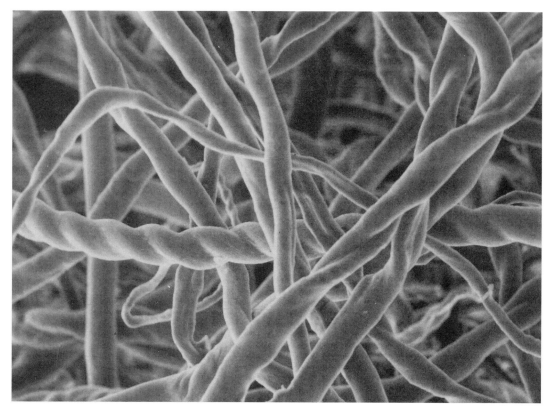

Fig. 4-8. Though all fibers are cellulose— whether from cotton, trees, or weeds—and bond naturally in water, their configuration can vary. Here is an electronmicrograph of cotton fibers, showing their typical spiral construction. Sufficiently trained and experienced, fiber microscopists can very often identify the plant source of fibers in a paper sheet.

WHY PAPER CAN BE MADE
CHAPTER FIVE

There's a bond greater than James (the ultra spy). It is the natural bond that holds fibers together in paper. The expansive prowess of spy fiction's Bond pales into anemia compared to the prowess of paper's natural bond. This bond is why paper can be made.

The bond is universal, unfailing, and active with what has been described as "the most abundant material on earth"—cellulose fibers. It is the key to the development of today's civilization (learning, culture, science) and has been the means to its own identification and elucidation.

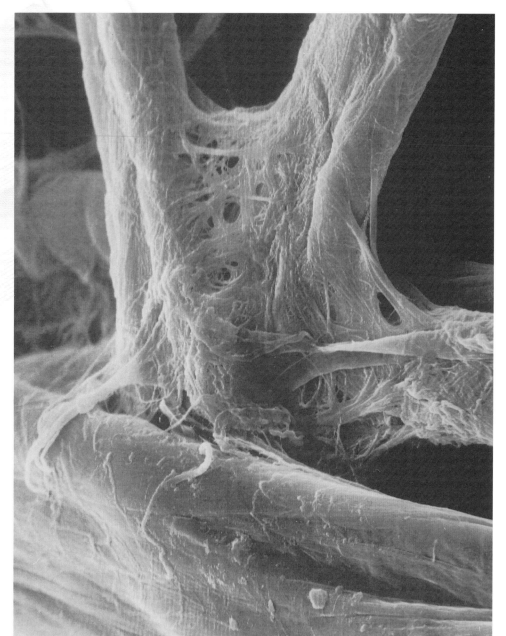

Fig. 5-1. This electronmicrograph shows several fibers naturally bonded within a filter paper. Wherever the three fibers touch, there is bonding. A network of fibrils (resulting from mechanically "beating" fibers) is seen between the two top fibers. At left center, fibrils lap over the bottom fiber. Fibrils create more bonded area and hence more strength. That is why fibrils are so exceedingly important.

The bond is powerful enough to remain the world-shaker of all time, yet is often worked and unworked by second-graders.

Is the phenomena really worthy of these words? The recording and diffusion of knowledge has to be the enabler for today's level of civilization and technology. The key to recording and diffusion has been paper. Paper is possible only because of the natural bond.

The bond is fantastic and simple—when two cellulose fibers meet in water (common and ordinary), wherever they touch, a natural bond occurs.

Man didn't make it, he just found out it happens.

And here is another amazing fact. Though it takes water (liquid moisture) to make it occur, once it has occurred, the more water taken away the stronger the bond becomes. It is a direct ratio. Measure the amount of water removed and a number can be put on the amount of strength induced in the bond between two fibers.

That is an amazing system. Take any piece of dry paper. Snap it between your hands. All that's holding it together is Nature saying, "Hey little fibers! Wherever you are touching a friend, hang on." That is strength.

Strength is an amazing and manipulatable factor with the fibers. First, the strength of the bond is the strength of paper. Strength comes from where one fiber touches another. Get more of one fiber to touch another and you have more strength. Consequently, the strength of a sheet is the sum of the bonded area within the sheet, which scientists can measure.

Part of the reason for the "papermaker's shake" (a side-to-side and back-and-forth movement of the hand mold after it has been lifted from the vat) is to get more of each fiber touching another.

This now takes us back to the fibrils in the previous chapter. Are they just an interesting and amazing phenomenon? No, they are vital in the papermaker's manipulations and used every day. If the fiber can be brushed with a steel bar, the little filbrils can be made to stick out from the main fiber, or the outer layers of fibrils can be splayed. In each case, more surface is exposed to make more total bonding surface available, which in turn makes more strength. The brushing of the fiber is called beating. Hand papermakers do it mostly with Hollander type beaters. Commercial mills additionally use disc refiners and "Jordans" in fiber preparation.

Therefore, this tiny bit of matter—a fibril—which just comes into view at 30 or 40 thousand times magnification, is a huge player in civilization's development and maintenance.

Some papers might include a bit of strength-increasing additive, but the increase would be so

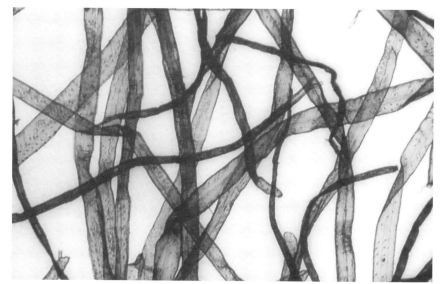

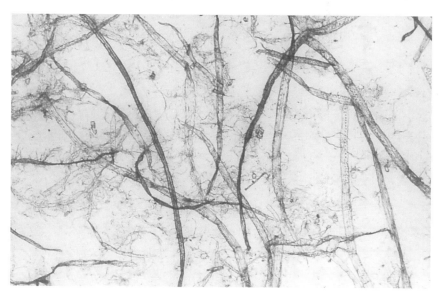

Figs. 5-2 and 5-3. Beating makes fibrils available for added bonding area. Compare the unbeaten fibers in the upper micrograph to the beaten fibers in the lower micrograph.

incremental an instrument would be required to measure it.

The bond is user friendly. Anyone who can put their hands on cellulose fibers and water can work it, unwork it, then rework it, continuing as long as they want to handle fibers and water. They might be age three or 83, in a modern paper mill or a pioneer kitchen. The bond works anywhere on any date.

And it can easily be unworked. If you don't want

the fibers to hang together, put them in water. As sure as the bond got stronger by removal of water, it will get weaker by the addition of water. Again, it's a direct ratio. That's why anyone who can put dry paper in water can unmake paper; that is, turn paper back into a batch of individual unconnected fibers (pulp). But even when totally water-soaked, some bond remains where fibers are touching. Consequently, total disconnection requires mechanical agitation, easily provided by a blender.

The same fibers can then be reconnected by redepositing them singly on each other in layers on a screen. They can then be dried back into paper. This is recycling. It's about as easy and simple as falling off a log (which is about as big a bundle of cellulose fibers as can be found). Paper must be as recyclable a material as there is.

Anyone can become aware of the bond's might and ubiquitous nature—simply go to your library and look at how much knowledge and information is on paper. All that paper is one fantastic batch of individual bonds. Or look at the most high-tech item in your house. Paper, as the recorder and diffuser of knowledge (even the directions on how to use it), made it possible.

If you feel the ease and simplicity of operating this amazing bond is overstated, simply tear up a 2″ square of paper, put it in a blender with enough water to just cover the blades, run the blender for 20 seconds (you now have single, unattached fibers in water), and slowly pour the water and fiber onto any kind of sieve (screen, strainer, dish cloth, fabric, etc.) so the fibers are left in a group touching each other. Now try to lift some fibers immediately—the bond will be so weak the fibers between your fingers will let loose of the others. But let the fiber mass dry completely and lift some fibers. The whole mass will likely rise with them. You have just seen for yourself the growth of strength of the natural bond. And nature did it all.

To paraphrase a familiar verbal icon—"Yes Virginia, there is a bond greater than James."

Fig. 5-4. A laboratory beater. The bars, visible under the hood, rotate. Fibers in slurry form go round and round in the tub. As they pass between the bars and an underlying metal bedplate, they are repeatedly macerated. The bars and bedplate separation can be varied, providing lighter or more severe beating.

Fig. 5-5. Fibers, as pulp, go round and round in this Hollander type beater. They pass under the hood on the right where they are forced between a metal bedplate and metal bars on a revolving cylinder.

PERMANENT AND ARCHIVAL HANDMADE PAPERS

CHAPTER SIX

Is it acid free?
Is it lignin-free?
Is it "permanent" or "archival"?

These are questions on many tongues these days,
especially in regard to the "memories" field.
Your "memories" are no doubt better off if the
answer to these questions is "Yes."
Let's talk about permanence and archival (acid-
free) paper in general, then about "memories" concerns specifically, and finally about
whether or not you can make your handmade
papers suitable for use with memories.

Permanence and Archival

First, there are, of course, no circumstances under which any paper is permanent. Regardless of how permanent or archival a paper is said to be, (a) a single spark can obliterate it, (b) a serious heat surge nearby can significantly alter its longevity, (c) light spectra from bulb or sun will age it, (d) a broken water pipe or a faucet left running can be its death knell, (e) autos passing your open window can reduce its longevity, (f) vermin around your house can eat it, (g) mold and fungi are hazards. To say nothing of a two-year-old run amok.

All of the above paper predators don't give two hoots as to whether or not paper is permanent or archival or pure groundwood (lignin-loaded).

So the first thing to understand in relation to permanence and archival (and therefore acid-free) is that the framework of reference for these terms is restricted to just one area of paper's total hazard environment.

Second, the permanence field is certainly not as "pat" as often portrayed. The field is far from technologically conquered. There are huge vagaries in paper survival. Witness several of my personal encounters.

Encounter 1. I have a fragment of paper that was underwater for 250 years. It was brought up from a shipwreck about a mile off Cape Kennedy. Though saturated in sea water for more than two and a half centuries, the paper today is almost pristine. It has a couple of oxidation spots. Exactly opposite is papyrus, which is certainly non-pure cellulose fiber. It survives well for centuries in desert dryness.

Encounter 2. While replacing a basement window in our home in the 1960s, I came across a newspaper stuffed in the void of a foundation block. It was a Milwaukee newspaper dated 1943. This is newsprint—very likely 100% groundwood (lignin-loaded). After 20 years in the cement block, it was in near excellent condition, hardly any fading. At a subsequent

This fragment of paper was underwater for at least 250 years. Other than a few rust stains, it is in near-pristine condition.

demonstration, I recycled the newspaper into handmade sheets. These are still in my possession (1998). They have been kept in a notebook in sheet protectors. They have faded some, but not a whole lot. This is after 50 years.

Encounter 3. This encounter taught me something about the durability of the cellulose fiber. You agree with me if you think that survival for 30 million years means durability. During my years at The Institute of Paper Chemistry, I showed an Australian friend a sheet of paper made from 11,000-year-old fibers pulped from an underground "forest" which extends under Appleton, Wisconsin, from the shores of Green Bay. The implication was that "Yanks" had all types of wonders that "Aussies" could only dream of. A short while later, I received my comeuppance. It was a handsheet from my Australian friend. It was made from a tree scientifically dated at 30 million years of age. It had been found in a coal mine. An accompanying note stated regret that, as usual, the Yanks were in second place. If you want to read about the tree, the scientific paper reporting it can be found in the October 1963 issue of the German journal, *Holzforschung*. The fibers, 30 million years later, look nice and white in paper which is now over 30 years old and is exhibited on a wall in my home. The paper has had no "permanence" treatment.

One concludes from these encounters that while acid-free permanence and archival treatments are certainly worthwhile, they are equally not the whole answer. Maybe (a) duplicating the conditions of the cement block void in my home's foundation, or (b) keeping paper immersed in sea water, or (c) duplicating the conditions of soil in an Australian coal mine would be equally well.

Memories Concerns

For keeping memories, papers offer more hope of longevity if they are acid-free, i.e. permanent or archival. Essentially, this means the pH level, which is a measurable quality, is in the immediate vicinity of 7.5. Readings lower than 7.0 are acid, higher are alkaline. Papermaking conditions that would normally lead to an acid reading (below 7.0 pH), can be treated to render a satisfactory pH reading by having an acid buffer included in the pulp, or inserted after the paper has been made. The buffer, usually calcium carbonate, will also provide protection from possible acid contamination after the sheet is made. The capacity for such protection is finite.

Finally, in relation to safeguarding memories, it should be remembered, as pointed out above, that preservation means awareness of paper-degrading factors other than acidity.

Can You Make Your Handmade Paper Safe For Memories?

Yes. Tools provided by modern science make it possible for the home papermaker to make paper that can be used for memories.

Science provides pulp that is acid-free or permanent or archival. Science also provides tools to buffer any pulp against destructive action by acid. One such tool is calcium carbonate. It can be added in the blender or in the vat. The other tools are solutions which can be sprayed on a sheet after the sheet is dried.

How to Make Memories-Safe Paper

There are three methods.

Method 1. Using recycled or new pulp, make paper as you always do. When the paper is dry, spray it with a commercial buffering solution such as Wei T'o. Your paper is then within the pH range usually ascribed to permanent or archival paper. Solutions are available from archival catalogs and from Greg Markim, Inc.

Method 2. Add calcium carbonate to pulp made by recycling any paper, or to new pulp (if it is not acid-free). It can be added while pulp is being dispersed or paper recycled in the blender, or in the vat. Make sure that your supplier includes directions with the calcium carbonate. Follow them exactly. The calcium carbonate will automatically bring your papermaking system into a pH level within the permanent and archival range.

Method 3. Buy acid-free pulp. But then make sure your water, couch sheets or felts, and any additives are all acid-free. You can use distilled water, which is generally not in the acid pH range. Ask suppliers about pH of their products. For instance, blotter couch sheets from Greg Markim, Inc. are in the archival pH range when they are shipped.

Get a pH testing pen or tape. It will let you keep track of the pH of your paper and the paper you are planning to recycle. For memory-book paper, it is better to recycle paper that has the right pH level. Testing pens are available from archival supply catalogs or from Greg Markim, Inc. listed in the Appendix.

But note this: Even if you don't care a fig about any of the above and have never heard of acid-free, permanence, archival, or lignin, the paper you make is not going to fall apart tomorrow, next week, or even probably for years. Nor will it cause your memory materials to fade immediately or get brittle next month. Indeed, much of such paper will outlast the people who made it.

Paper used in the world of commerce (letters, envelopes, reports, etc.) have seldom, if ever, been rated archival or had a pH of 7.5. But if you go to an older business in your area and ask to see some of their earliest files (which have likely been kept in nonarchival manila folders), you will probably find much of the paper in quite reasonable condition.

So, in the face of the permanence and acid-free information onslaught, don't panic. Just keep the information in perspective and apply it when it is appropriate because of a paper's emotional or monetary value.

RECYCLING

CHAPTER SEVEN

CHAPTER SEVEN

"Waste Paper Is Not Waste Fiber"

In this book, "recycling" means taking paper, turning it into wet pulp with water and a blender, and making the wet pulp back into handmade paper.

Recycling is predicated on the fact that paper is dried pulp. If pulp, when dried, becomes paper, then obviously when wetted, paper becomes pulp.

This book seeks to open your mind and eyes to the vast store of invaluable, expensive papermaking components lying idle in the nation's stores of waste paper.

To think of these fibers as "used" is the folly of thinking of a new car driven home from a dealer's showroom as "used" and throwing it away. Hundreds of in-depth research projects costing millions of dollars have been done on recycled fibers. People who believe recycled fibers are some unknown, best-to-ignore product are simply victims of severely limited knowledge.

A simple fact needs recognition: waste paper is not waste fiber.

The paper industry's finest treasures (fibers, additives, color, etc.) are lying in waste paper piles and are available to hand papermakers absolutely free. The beautiful three- or four-color soft-sized handmade sheet that can be made in four minutes by recycling would take days, money, and equipment to make if the papermaker started with new white pulp.

By recycling, the "waste" papers at left were turned into the handmade sheet at right.

How

Recycling is done in three steps. 1. Tear up paper and put it in a blender with water; 2. Run the blender for 30 seconds or less, turning the paper into pulp; and 3. Make the pulp into a handmade sheet. With those simple steps, you have recycled.

How much paper and how much water should be put in the blender? It can vary, but a rule of thumb is to tear 3/4 of an 8½″ x 11″ sheet of paper into small pieces. Put the pieces in a blender with 2 to 2½ cups of water. This amount will produce a new 5″ x 8″ sheet of handmade paper. From this basic formula, you can work up or down for the ratio of paper and water in the blender.

Why

Waste paper is not waste fiber. Every different type of paper you recycle gives you a different type of handmade sheet. This happens because there is a difference between pulp and furnish. Pulp is simply fibers. Furnish is fibers plus additives. Furnish is a recipe of fibers, sizing, fillers, optical brighteners, etc.

Not much paper is made of just fibers. If it were, it would be waterleaf (blotter paper). Almost all paper is made from a furnish.

With new fibers you have to find, buy, and properly add all the necessary additives. When you recycle, all the additives have been selected, added, and paid for—no work, no expense, and ready *now*. When recycling existing paper you already have a furnish.

Industry spends a lot of time, money, and research, plus testing and evaluating to arrive at the right furnish. To you, it's free in your wastebasket as you read this.

By recycling you can make handmade paper with every furnish ever created by the paper industry. Each furnish is different and makes different paper. Each different sheet you recycle will produce a different (slightly or radically) handmade sheet.

"But the fibers are used," you say. So are "new" fibers—they are pulped, put in water, run out on a screen and dried into pulp, packaged, sold, recycled into wet pulp in a blender or hydrapulper, run in a mixer to make a furnish, then run out on a screen as paper. By that time, they have been "used" too.

Cotton rag fibers are probably the most used. They have been woven into thread, woven again as thread into fabric, handled while sewn into clothes, cycled through wearing and washing, heated and reheated in ironing, re-isolated as individuals by malicious assault of a beater, and made into wet pulp and run out on a screen in dry lap form. Then before use, recycled in a blender or hydrapulper from dry lap into wet pulp. That is used! That is recycled!

If you don't worry about using 100% cotton fiber because it is used, why worry about any other fiber used only once?

Remember—waste paper is not waste fiber. Paper is waste because it cannot be used again as paper, but the *fibers* are not waste. Their useful life has hardly started. Not only is waste paper not waste fiber, but science shows that for some paper qualities, recycled fibers are superior to new fibers. Recycled fibers have been studied inside and out in hundreds of research projects. The paper industry is breaking its back and bottom line to use recycled fibers more.

Is handmade paper made of recycled fibers permanent and archival? If one wants to spend the money, recycled fibers can be made as archival and permanent as new fibers upon which similar money has been spent.

So not only is recycling okay, in my opinion it is advisable. Decorative and artistic papermaking would be severely limited were vast and varied art and decorative resources not easily available immediately and free through recycling.

What

All and any paper can be recycled. If it can't be recycled, it isn't paper. Recycle everything to find out what it is that you like to recycle.

Just like new fibers, fibers to recycle run the gamut from cheap to the world's finest. You can judge somewhat which are which by who is using the fibers (banks, culture-conscious organizations, image-conscious entities, etc.), or what they are being used for (printed programs for operas, anniversaries of corporations or organizations, personal stationery of elected officials, etc.).

At the bottom of quality and cost are groundwood fibers, amply available as newsprint. At the top of the line are cotton and certain wood fibers pulped by advanced pulping technology, bleached for whiteness and/or further purification, and perhaps in a furnish including opacifiers, optical brighteners, etc.

* **Newsprint**: With newsprint you can make handmade paper that might contain a recycled comic strip (a big hit with kids) or a newspaper story about friends. Its short fibers are good for watermarking. Newsprint makes a nice gray sheet. One disadvantage is that the ink released from the fibers makes a rather dirty film or scum which gets on the papermaking equipment and can turn white papermaking screens gray. The ink problem can be avoided by cutting off and using only the unprinted margins. Always clean all the equipment thoroughly after each use.

* **Home or Business Communications Paper:** This covers a broad spectrum of good-looking, highly acceptable fibers in good furnishes. They offer colors as well as shades of white. Hold sheets to light to see if a watermark tells you the cotton content. Avoid printed ink effects by cutting away and using only the unprinted areas. Or use the inked sections to give a visual texture and color to handmade sheets.

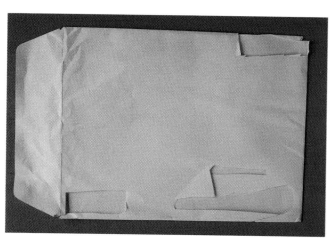

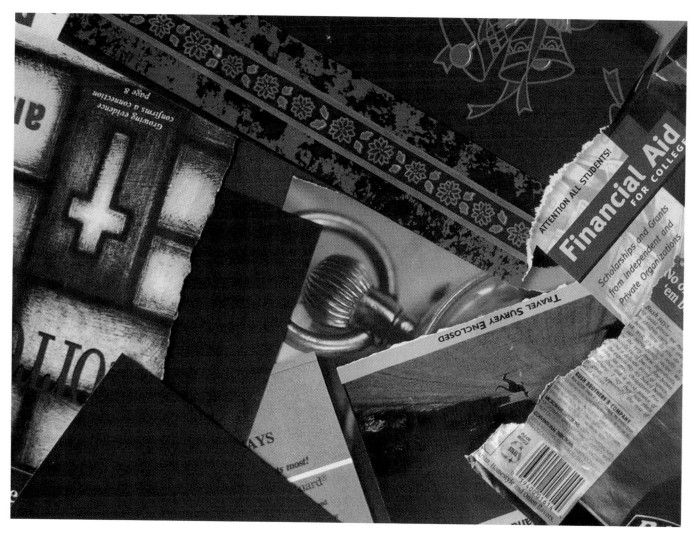

* **Envelopes**: These can be the backbone of white pulp supply. They are generally clean and range into the highest whiteness and the best fibers. They offer a wide range of colored fibers. Color from ink is bountiful from "security" envelopes where the inside of the envelope is printed with a colored pattern. Recycle glued flaps. Large envelopes often offer long fibers for strength. For pure white or colored pulp, use only the unprinted areas.

* **Bags**: Many bags offer long fibers for strength. Custom bags from upscale department stores can offer great and unusual colors. Plain brown sacks offer a great natural earth-tone background for some botanicals. White grocery bags are the result of very expensive long-fiber, bleached pulp. A short presoak before blending helps but is not necessary. The long fibers will tend to "flock" (see Glossary) in handmade sheets.

* **Wrapping Papers**: These are a happy hunting ground for colors, unusual inks, and foils. They are excellent to use for mottling (page 52).

* **Magazines**: Slick and shiny pages of any publication can be recycled. The fiber quality varies. Magazine covers can offer unusual possibilities for handmade sheets.

* **Colored Papers**: These are dyed fibers and therefore a source of colored pulp for colored handmade

papers. Because of poor fiber and dyes that run, I totally avoid "construction" paper when recycling.

* **Superlative Fibers**: For superlative fibers, look for superlative uses. The paper used for programs for concerts, drama, opera, etc. is likely to be very high quality. The same is usually true of invitations to landmark events and anniversary programs and publications.

* **Christmas Harvest**: Harvest colored envelopes for dyed fibers; cards with lots of metallic ink; Christmas wrapping paper with color, heavy ink, or foil components; illustrations from cards to be surface embedded on next year's cards; ribbons, strings, etc. for inclusion in next year's cards.

Additives

Additives are whatever is in a sheet other than fibers. Their purpose is to give the sheet specific characteristics. Additives are what makes one sheet different from another. Common additives include sizes, optical brighteners, opacifiers, fillers, etc. In terms of chemicals, the commercial paper industry is second only to the food industry as a customer of the chemical industry. This points up the advantage of recycling—additives in paper recycled become part of the handmade sheet.

PART 2

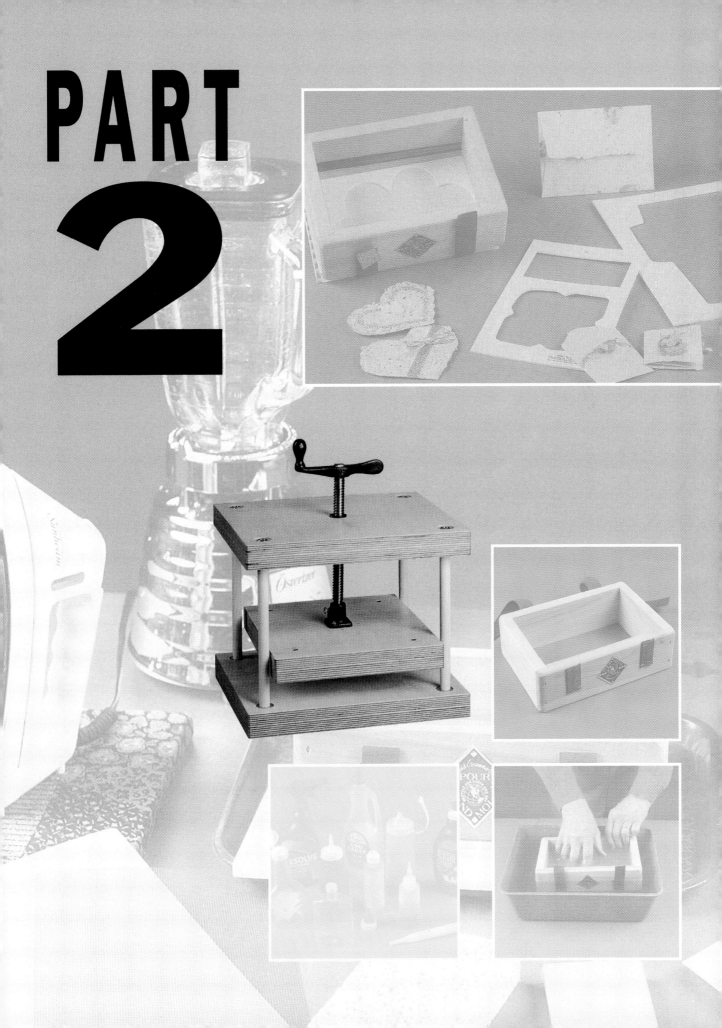

EQUIPMENT AND MATERIALS

CHAPTER EIGHT

Pour and Dip Hand Molds

Dard Hunter, founder of the Dard Hunter Paper Museum and master paper historian, believed the first sheet of paper was likely made with a pour hand mold. A pour mold is placed in a vat of water and pulp is poured into it. A dip mold is dipped into pulp in a vat. A pour mold generally has higher deckle walls than a dip mold and can move easily from one type or color of sheet to another. A dip mold can rapidly produce many sheets of the same type. A pour mold requires less preparation and cleanup than a dip mold. A pour mold can make sheets not practical for a dip mold, and is, consequently, more versatile.

I believe that anyone capable of lifting a pour mold out of water and holding it level while water drains will make a near-perfect sheet the first time they try.

Pour mold.

Dip mold.

Pour Mold Procedure

1. Put 3″ or 4″ of water in a vat large enough to hold the pour mold.
2. Prepare enough pulp for a single handmade sheet. (Recycling recipes: For a 5½″ x 8½″ mold, recycle 3/4 of a 8½″ x 11″ sheet of paper with 2 to 2½ cups water. For an 8½″ x 11″ mold, recycle 1¼ to 1½ sheets of 8½″ x 11″ paper in 3 to 3½ cups of water.)
3. Place the mold in the vat.
4. Pour the pulp into the mold's deckle.
5. Agitate the pulp for even dispersion in the deckle.
6. Lift the mold out of the water and hold it level while the water drains.
7. Remove the deckle. Couch the sheet from the screen, press it, and let it dry.

Dip Mold Procedure

1️⃣ Select a vat large enough to accommodate the mold and a hand on each side.

2️⃣ Pour prepared pulp into the vat until it is deep enough for the mold to be dipped totally beneath the pulp's surface. Actually, deeper is better.

3️⃣ Grasping both sides, dip the mold into the pulp vertically, flatten to horizontal beneath the pulp's surface, then lift it out of the pulp.

4️⃣ Remove the deckle (with or without a draining period) from the mold. Couch the sheet off the screen, press it, and let it dry. Repeat. Note the thickness of each sheet. When the sheets get too thin, add more pulp to the vat. With very small vats, this can be after as few as every two sheets.

NOTE: The "papermaker's shake" was part of a journeyman hand papermaker's skill. It was vital for certain qualities and characteristics of professional sheets. In general, it entailed shaking the hand mold forward and backward and from side-to-side after it had been lifted from the vat and while the pulp drained. The shake can be done with either pour or dip molds.

Building a Simple Pour Hand Mold

A pour mold can be built to any dimensions desired. Building it to the dimensions suggested here will produce handmade sheets approximately 5½″ x 8½″.

MATERIALS

+ 2 pieces of wood 1″ x 3″ x 9½″
+ 2 pieces of wood 1″ x 1″ x 9½″
+ 2 pieces of wood 1″ x 3″ x 5½″
+ 2 pieces of wood 1″ x 1″ x 5½″
+ Hardware cloth 5½″ x 9½″
+ Screen 5½″ x 9½″ (purchased commercial papermaking screen or nonmetal window screen)

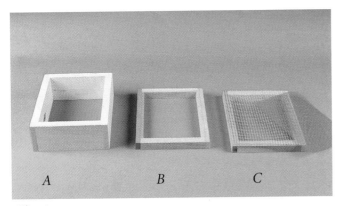

Fig. 1

Fig. 2. A and B above can be held tightly together with easily removable Velcro straps.

❶ Nail the four 1″ x 3″ pieces together in a frame (Fig 1-A).
❷ Nail the four 1″ x 1″ pieces together in a frame (Fig 1-B).
❸ Cover the 1″ x 1″ piece frame with hardware cloth (Fig 1-C).
❹ The 1″ x 3″ pieces form the deckle. The 1″ x 1″ pieces in Fig. 1-C form the papermaking screen support, which can also serve as the drain rack. To assemble, place the screen on the support's hardware cloth, then place the deckle on top of the screen. You'll need to secure the screen support tightly against the deckle for sheet formation, but loosen it to remove the screen support and new sheet after sheet formation. Use clasps, clamps, or straps.

In addition to a pour or dip mold, you'll need the following items.

+ Blender for preparing pulp slurry.
+ Vat—dishpan large enough to accommodate the hand mold.
+ Drain pan—tray, cookie sheet, etc.
+ Drain rack—anything a papermaking screen and new sheet can be laid on for draining. Sometimes the drain rack is the papermaking screen support of the hand mold.
+ Cover screen—a piece of non-metallic window screen a bit bigger than the sheet you're making.
+ Sponge.
+ Couch sheets—absorbent material in pieces larger than the sheet being made. Thick paper toweling or blotter sheets work well (see page 39).
+ Press bar—any piece of flat metal, wood, or plastic, or book encased in a plastic sack (see page 41).
+ Iron for drying.
+ Pulp gun—turkey baster, mustard bottle, etc. (see page 40).

Nothing from this list is difficult to find in your home or garage except the hand mold. (You can make your own simple hand mold by following the directions on this page.) Ready-to-use kits or individual items such as papermaking screens can be purchased at many craft stores. Some kits contain everything except the vat, tray, iron, and blender. See the Appendix for vendors.

Double Deckles

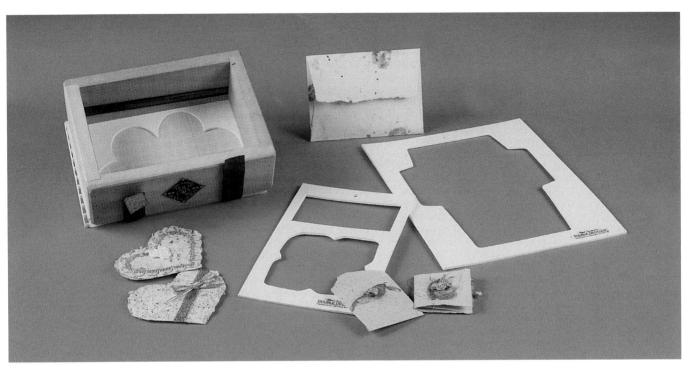

The envelope double deckle at right makes the envelope above it. The double deckle at center makes (simultaneously) the small folded note and matching envelope in the foreground. A "heart card" double deckle in the hand mold makes the heart cards at lower left.

Placed on top of the papermaking screen, a deckle determines the shape and size of the sheet. If a piece of flat material with an image cut out of it is placed on top of the screen but under the deckle, the water will have to go through the area that is cut out. That will put the fibers there also. So the sheet formed will be the size and shape of the area cut out of the flat material. This makes the flat material with its cutout, another deckle, giving the hand mold a "double deckle." The second deckle can be made with something like foam board, wood, plastic, or even metal. There are ready-made double deckles available from Greg Markim, Inc. and other suppliers.

Couching Materials

In papermaking, couch means taking the new wet sheet off the papermaking screen. Too weak to be lifted off by hand, the sheet must be coaxed off with the aid of some material. This is called a couch material, felt, or a couch sheet. In the past, felts of a special wool and weave were used in hand papermaking mills. These are no longer available, nor is the training on how to use them.

Hand papermakers today must find substitutes. Those replicating the old hand papermakers try a variety of blankets, etc. Any stable material that is absorbent works well. Couch sheets—blotter paper—are perhaps the most efficient, easiest, and surest to work. They are inexpensive and can be dried and reused. Precut professional papermakers' blotter couch sheets are available from Greg Markim, Inc. General desk blotters might be found at office supply stores. These will have to be cut and might not be as satisfactory for papermaking. If colored, they might bleed onto wet sheets.

Interestingly, new sheets can be couched off the screen onto most any solid surface, as shown in board drying on page 100.

Pulp Guns

A pulp gun is vital in making art and decoration with fibers. In this book, a pulp gun is any container from which pulp slurry can be squirted (shot), poured, or shaken in bursts or in a sprinkle.

A common gun is a turkey baster. Also common are plastic containers with spouts or nozzles such as mustard dispensers, plastic cosmetic containers, plastic shaving lotion bottles, syrup pour dispensers, plastic laboratory bottles with spouts that can be snipped off for smaller or larger openings. Easily made is a plastic soda bottle with a hole drilled in the cap.

Keep your eyes open for any kind of dispensing container and try it. Different effects can be produced by varying the thickness of the pulp slurries, the squirting force, and the angle at which the pulp is shot into or onto pulp or onto a bare screen (for pulp layering).

Drying Press

Pressing handmade paper is simply applying pressure to sheets to remove water. It can be simple and inexpensive or more complicated and very expensive. The method doesn't have much effect on the final result, as long as it's done right. But the more pressure applied, the more some sheet characteristics are enhanced.

"Simple" includes piling weights on top of the wet sheet of paper which has been placed between absorbent materials such as couch blotter sheets, paper towels, paper wipes, etc. The weight can be a stack of books or any heavy object (concrete or stone building blocks, pieces of metal, etc.).

"Expensive" gets into the field of commercial presses, ranging from the one shown, a Greg Markim two-ton easily portable screw press with a current price around $160, to hydraulic presses from other suppliers ranging up to and over $3,000.

Watch for presses made for other purposes which can be used for paper. A prime example is the coveted and now costly bookbinder's press.

Of course, you can build your own drying press. My previous book, *Paper by Kids*, shows an easily built, inexpensive press frame for use with a two-ton hydraulic auto jack available from any discount store ($10 to $12). It works beautifully.

Presses and pressing are another one of those great fields for creativity.

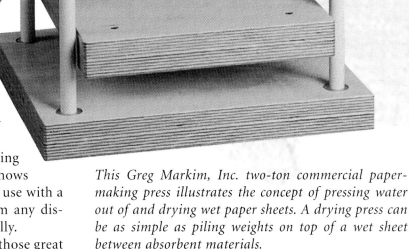

This Greg Markim, Inc. two-ton commercial paper-making press illustrates the concept of pressing water out of and drying wet paper sheets. A drying press can be as simple as piling weights on top of a wet sheet between absorbent materials.

New Pulp

If you choose to forgo the paper recycling process, you will need to find other sources for pulp fibers. Today's "start from scratch" papermakers are experimenting with getting fibers from many traditional and new plants. Traditional ones include Oriental plants such as gampi, mitsumata, and kozo whose fibers require special formation aids and sheet forming techniques. Also traditional are hemp, abaca, cotton rag, etc.

The easiest pulp to use and obtain is cotton linter, available in convenient packages at art and craft stores and from suppliers listed in the Appendix.

Wood fibers are most readily available to hand papermakers by recycling. Though tested by the commercial paper industry years ago, banana plant fibers have only recently entered hand papermaking. A variety of these pulps is available from the papermaking suppliers listed in the Appendix.

Several "specialty" pulps are available from Greg Markim, Inc. and other suppliers. These include cotton with scrubbed corn husk, cotton rag denim and khaki, and some synthetic and cellulose fiber blends. These pulps will make waterleaf (blotter) paper unless sizing is added.

Sizing

When recycling, some of the sizing in the paper you're recycling is residual in the "new" paper you're making.

If all the research on sizing were printed out, it would likely cover acres. Its basis is exceedingly scientific. Therefore, this presentation on sizing is meant to be only an opening of the door to the subject, plus some things you can do effectively without a Ph.D. in paper surface chemistry. Additionally, sources for commercial sizing are listed in the Appendix.

Sizing helps fibers—individually or as a paper structure—resist moisture and liquids. If not sized, fibers are hydrophyllic, like sponges and blotters. Papers made from just water and fiber (no additives) are blotters.

Fibers can be sized individually as part of the pulp before the sheet is made, or en masse as a formed sheet. The former is "internal" sizing, the latter is "external" sizing. For internal, sizing is put into the pulp. For external, sizing is applied to the sheet's surface or the sheet can be immersed in sizing (tub sizing). Deeper into the subject, there are variations and combinations.

Sizing is soft or hard or somewhere between. Soft sizing adds just a bit of moisture resistance. Hard adds a lot.

Being costly, sizing is introduced into paper in just the amount the paper's use demands. Because natural organic sizings increase the danger of continued chemical reaction and varmint attraction, the commercial paper industry has moved toward synthetic sizings.

In old European mills, sizing was animal glue obtained by boiling hides, horns, and hooves. It was applied by a version of tub sizing.

Sizing is not a simple process, because when put into pulp, most of it washes off the fibers during water drainage. To prevent this, scientists add a second agent which chemically bonds the sizing to the fibers. In the late 1800s, this agent was alum. But alum introduces continued deleterious chemical reaction with modern environmental elements. Synthetic sizings and agents are advantageously inert.

Given all this, can a hand papermaker size paper? Yes.

Wax is an excellent sizing and it's easy to get—free. One source is waxed sacks used by bakeries to send pastries home with customers. They look and feel "waxy." The wax has been processed for use in paper. It's easy to use the wax for sizing in hand papermaking.

Step 1. Tear up the waxed sack and soak it in hot water for 15 minutes. You can also use waxed paper, but it's a little harder to pulp in the blender.

Step 2. Run the soaked waxed sack pieces in a blender with hot water. (For a waxed sack equal to 3/4 of a 8½″ x 11″ sheet of paper, use 2½ to 3 cups of water.) Run the blender until there are no paper chunks visible.

Now you have 2½ to 3 cups of excellent liquid sizing. Using it is easy. Put some into the pulp in a pour hand mold or, for dip molds, put it in the pulp in the vat and mix well. You can put a little or a lot. For hard sizing use more, for soft sizing use less. (For our purposes, soft sizing is equal to that of general and business stationery and envelopes. Hard sizing is equal to good calligraphy paper.) For soft sizing, add one part waxed sack pulp to five parts general recycled pulp. For hard sizing, add equal parts waxed sack pulp and general recycled pulp. For even harder sizing, add three parts waxed sack pulp to one part general recycled pulp. For new pulp, and especially cotton (rag or linters), sizing will be a bit softer. The more pure a fiber, the harder it is to size.

A drop of colored water sitting on a sheet made partly with recycled wax sacks.

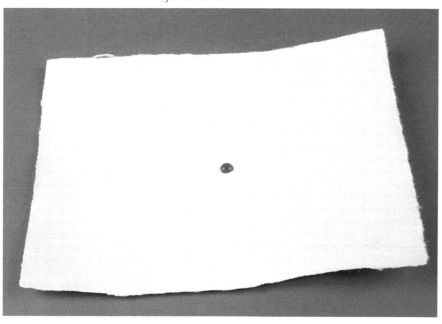

Starch is another sizing option. You can try corn starch (commonly used in cooking) or laundry starch. Neither of these seem to work well for sizing paper. They are not modified for paper requirements. Put in pulp, they mostly wash off during drainage. Even sprayed on a dry sheet, their effect is hard to detect without scientific instruments.

Try some experiments yourself. Dissolve some corn starch in water (try two heaping tablespoons per cup of water). Put this solution in a pan larger than the sheets you make by hand. Prepare enough to make the solution an inch deep in the pan. Now hold a fiber-tipped pen on the surface of a dry handmade sheet for five seconds. A circle of ink will spread from the pen's tip. Immerse the sheet in the starch solution and let it air dry. Hold the same fiber-tipped pen on the surface for five seconds. Compare the size of the two circles made before and after the sheet was in the starch. Is the second circle smaller than the first? If it is, the starch sizing worked. If it isn't noticeably smaller, the starch wasn't effective.

Also test spray starch by applying a fiber-tipped pen to an untreated dry handmade sheet. Then spray the sheet with spray starch, let the sheet dry, and apply the pen to the sheet again. Compare the size of the two ink circles. If the spray starch helped, the second ink circle should be smaller.

Testing for Sizing

Described above is a simple, informal test for sizing using a fiber-tipped pen. A water drop can provide a second test. Drop a small drop of water on the surface of a sheet. Watch and see how fast the water disappears into the sheet. The longer it takes the drop to absorb into the sheet, the better the sizing. These tests are simple and rudimentary. The results are not meant for scientific reports, but are informative for papermakers.

Other Sizing Possibilities

There are store-shelf products for making cellulose fibers in wood and fabrics water repellent. Will the products make cellulose fibers in paper water repellent? Apparently so. I experimented with four products: Scotch Gard Water Repellent, Green Street Fabric Stiffener, Thompson's Water Seal, and an exterior/interior clear gloss polyurethane. Each was used to spray a handmade sheet. After the sheets dried, I tested them with a drop of water and a fiber-tipped pen. Water was still visible on each sheet surface after an hour in the drop test. That is hard sized paper. The results weren't so consistent with the fiber-tipped pen. After two spot and script-writing tests on each sheet, I rated the products for hardness of sizing in the following order: Scotch Gard, polyurethane, Thompson's, and fabric stiffener. The Scotch Gard delivered the hardest sizing, but the others weren't far behind.

I make no evaluation on the economic, time and labor feasibility of any of these four products, nor do I recommend or discourage their use. This is simply a report of facts concerning the interaction of paper and products. If you use any of these products carefully read the instructions on the package.

Finally, sizings are made especially for paper and used in the commercial paper industry. They are available from several suppliers listed in the Appendix.

Summary

Wax is an excellent, easily available (waxed sacks or paper), easy-to-use, effective sizing. Starch in unmodified store-shelf form probably is not effective. Clear gelatin, often suggested, involves preparation and application procedures. Some spray products made for water repellence in other materials work with paper. No matter which you use, always read the labels.

BASIC TECHNIQUES
CHAPTER NINE

Preparing Pulp

For hand papermakers, preparing pulp means (a) getting an amount of new dry pulp or waste paper, (b) putting it in a blender with water, and (c) running the blender until the pulp or waste paper is dispersed into single fibers in the water. For some techniques, the blender is turned off early when recycling waste paper.

Some papermakers and most papermaking centers have a beater for pulp preparation or refining. But blenders will be a mainstay for most, and rightly so. For years I walked the laboratories of The Institute of Paper Chemistry and heard blenders whirring, dispersing experimental and exotic pulps.

How Much Water and Paper?

The answer comes from a basic rationale. Fibers are hydrophillic. In water, they swell like a sponge, requiring more room than when dry. Also, if they are to part from each other, more room is required than when hanging together. So there must be enough water to provide room for fiber-swelling and fiber movement away from each other. Enough water must be put in the blender to provide that kind of room. The more new pulp or waste paper put in, the more water is required.

This rationale develops into the following general formulas for pour and dip molds.

Pour Molds

❖ For 5½" x 8½" sheets, tear up 3/4 of an 8½" x 11" sheet and add 2 to 2½ cups of water.
❖ For 8½" x 11" sheets, tear up 1¼ to 1½ sheets of 8½" x 11" paper and add 3 to 3½ cups of water.
❖ For other sizes, follow the general rule of tearing up a piece of paper that is a bit larger than the measurements of the pour mold's deckle. Smaller pieces of paper which together equal sizes listed above can be torn up instead of single pieces.

Dip Molds

For dip molds, pulp preparation aims at a pulp thickness in the vat, not at a size of sheet to be made. For a pulp consistency providing sheets of general communication paper thickness, use the following.

Tear up one 8½" x 11" sheet and add 4 cups of water. Run the blender. Pour the recycled pulp into a vat. Repeat until there are 3 or more inches of pulp in the vat. After two or three sheets have been dipped, add pulp to the vat according to the following ratio: tear up one 8½" x 11" sheet and add 3 cups of water. Run the blender. Add the pulp to the vat.

New Pulp

The above is for recycling waste paper. For new pulp, follow the directions provided with the pulp. If no directions are provided, experiment. Estimate the amount of pulp needed. Add plenty of water. Run the blender. Form a sheet.

For a pour mold, if the sheet is too thick, take part of the pulp off the screen. Lower the mold in the water again. Disperse the remaining pulp in the deckle and form a new sheet. Repeat the removal or addition of pulp process until you have the right thickness. The amount of pulp removed or added will indicate how much dry pulp is about the right amount to start with.

For dip molds, if the formed sheet is too thick, either add water to the vat or with a strainer, remove pulp. Dip a new sheet. Continue this process until the vat's pulp consistency is right.

Final Comments

For paper recycling, tearing up thicker paper requires the addition of more water. For blender operation, start the blender at a slow speed. When the paper and water stop jumping up and down, change to a higher speed. This will prevent water from spraying out from under the lid when the blender is started.

Thick and Thin Sheets

The sheet thickness can be controlled by varying the ratio of fiber to water in the pulp slurry. With pour molds, thickness can be controlled easily and precisely. With dip molds, it's a bit tricky.

Controlling Thickness with Pour Molds

When recycling, the following provides precise control. Tear and blend a piece of paper the same length and width as the deckle (see Preparing Pulp above for the amount of water to use). The new sheet made from that pulp will be of the same thickness as the paper recycled. This provides a reference point. To make a new sheet twice as thick, recycle twice the paper, adjusting the amount of water added in the blender. For a sheet half as thick, recycle half as much paper.

When starting with new pulp, preciseness is not as easy. As stated above, you can either guess at how much dry pulp to blend, see what thickness results, and work from that as a reference point, or with an appropriate scale, weigh out an estimated amount of dry pulp, disperse it in a blender, see what thickness results from that amount and work mathematically from that as a reference point.

Controlling Thickness with Dip Molds

With dip molds, you must alter the thickness of the slurry in the vat to change the thickness of paper. Adding pulp will make the next sheets thicker. Adding water or removing pulp with a strainer will make the next sheets thinner.

The thickness fact to remember with the dip mold is that each time you make a sheet of paper, you remove pulp from the vat. The fiber stays out but the water runs back in. Therefore, the slurry in the vat is thinner and the following sheet will be thinner unless you replace the amount of fiber taken out.

Basic Steps for Hand Papermaking

These basic steps are the foundation of all pour mold sheetmaking. No matter what technique or project you choose, you will be referred back to these basic steps. To help you locate these pages easily, we've colored the edges blue.

The directions below are for pour molds because they offer more options, are easier to use, and are more flexible and less work. Though not shown, pour molds with the deckle and bottom hinged will work well also. Pour molds work with all techniques. If you are using a dip mold, refer to the instructions on page 50. Prepare the pulp (see page 45).

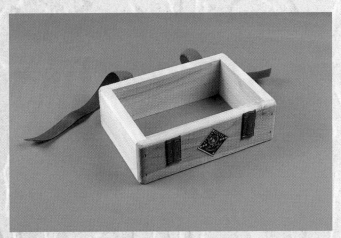

STEP 1. Place the mold upside-down on a flat surface.

STEP 2. Lay the papermaking screen on the mold. Lay the drain rack grid on the screen.

Step 3. Pull the straps tightly across the drain rack. Push the long straps firmly against the short straps on the mold's side.

Step 4. Lower the mold at a slanted angle into the water in a vat (tub or dishpan). The water must be deep enough to come within 1/4″ of the mold's top.

Step 5. Pour pulp into the deckle.

Step 6. By wiggling your fingers or stirring with a plastic spoon, spread the pulp evenly in the water in the deckle.

Step 7. Lift the mold out of the water. Hold it level and let all the water drain.

Step 8. Set the mold down in a drain pan (cookie tray, etc.). Loosen the straps.

Step 9. Lift the deckle up from over the screen and drain rack. If the screen lifts with the deckle, separate the two with your fingernail or a knife blade.

Step 10. Having set the deckle aside, carefully put a cover (protective) screen over the new sheet.

Step 11. Press a sponge firmly down on the cover screen. Wring the sponge. Press again. Continue until the sponge removes no more water.

Step 12. Carefully lift a corner of the cover screen. Peel the screen off slowly. If the sheet comes up with the screen, try the other corners.

Step 15. Place one hand on the middle and one hand at the corner of the screen. Slowly lift the corner and peel off the screen. Slide one hand back as the other lifts. If the sheet comes up with the screen, press down hard on each corner and try lifting at each.

Step 13. Pick up the papermaking screen with the new sheet. Turn it over. Place it—new sheet down—on a dry couch sheet (absorbent material). The new sheet will be between the screen and couch sheet.

Step 16. Put a dry couch sheet over the new sheet.

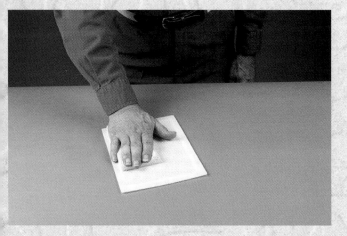

Step 14. Firmly press a sponge down all over the screen's surface. Wring the sponge and press again.

Step 17. With a press bar (flat piece of wood, plastic, or metal), press down hard over the entire surface of the couch sheet.

Step 18. Take off the top couch sheet. Carefully lift one corner of the new sheet. (If the new sheet is too weak, repeat Step 17 with a dry couch sheet.)

Step 21. Admire your new sheet.

Heat drying generally causes curl and cockle. Moving the iron's edge against the curl while at the same time lifting the paper against the curl can help create a flat sheet.

Heat drying delivers paper immediately, but drying without heat is better for some paper qualities and delivers a better looking sheet. For more quality, dry your paper slowly under pressure. After Step 19, place the paper between two dry couch sheets. Use a press if you have one or place the sheets between two boards and stack weight on the top board (books, cement blocks). After 20 minutes, exchange the wet couch sheets for dry ones. After two hours, change couch sheets again and leave the paper under pressure for five or six hours, or, better yet, overnight. After this, if it's not too thick, the paper should be dry. If not, keep exchanging couch sheets until it is. (Curing occurs, as well as drying, during time under pressure. Literally, the longer under pressure, the more some qualities will be enhanced.)

Step 19. Peel the new sheet off the couch sheet.

If Using a Dip Mold

For Steps 1 through 3, papermakers using dip molds can simply prepare their molds according to manufacturer's directions. In Step 4, dip the mold into a vat full of pulp, lift it out as in Step 7, lift off the deckle for Steps 8 and 9, and rejoin the pour procedures in Step 10.

Some techniques involving procedures while pulp is in the pour mold's deckle will be very difficult, maybe impossible, for the dip mold. However, really ardent dip mold users will undoubtedly try. Best wishes.

Step 20. Place the new sheet on an ironing board or on a cloth-covered flat surface. Place a thin cloth over the sheet. Iron the new sheet dry with an iron turned up to maximum heat (no steam).

ARTISTIC AND DECORATIVE
TECHNIQUES
CHAPTER TEN

Artistic and decorative techniques can take you far beyond plain white or colored sheets. With these techniques, you will explore many materials, styles, and moods.

The techniques provide great opportunity for creativity, imagination, and self expression on both craft and artistic levels. They can likely accommodate the highest level of artistic talent. Pick one that strikes your fancy and go.

Mottled Surface

Mottled surfaces show small and/or large chunks of undefibered paper. This is the result of turning the blender off early in the recycling process. Blending many different colored papers or a paper printed with many different colored inks results in many different colored chunks and a striking handmade paper surface results. It is one of the easiest art/decorative techniques.

This is an excellent prospect for a mottled surface. The state of the paper during recycling can be seen through the blender's sides.

This sheet's surface is mottled with portions of torn photographs.

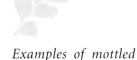

Examples of mottled
surface sheets.

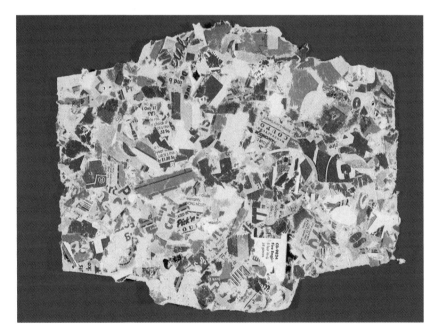

STEP 1. Select paper for recycling. Select many different colored papers and/or paper bearing brilliant, different colored inks.

STEP 2. Tear the paper into pieces and put the pieces in the blender.

NOTE. Pieces showing up later on the handmade paper's surface might be small, large, or both, but the pieces will never be larger than those put into the blender. In other words, don't tear the paper into pieces smaller than you want to appear on your handmade sheet.

STEP 3. Add water to the blender until it is 3/4 to 7/8 full.

STEP 4. Run the blender at midspeed two to three seconds.

Step 5. Do the basic hand papermaking Steps 1 through 4.

STEP 6. Pour the recycled pulp into the hand mold.

STEP 7. Tear up more paper—1/4 as much paper as you tore up before—and add it to a cup of water in the blender. Blend for 15 seconds or until there are no chunks visible. Add this second batch of pulp to the pulp already in the hand mold.

STEP 8. Keeping the hand mold low in the water, with the water in the deckle as deep as possible, agitate the pulp vigorously.

NOTE: Agitation should be vigorous. Large pieces of paper, like long papermaking fibers, tend to flock. Much water and agitation in the deckle will help prevent flocking.

STEP 9. Do the basic hand papermaking Steps 7 through 20.

NOTE: Large paper chunks tend to rise to the top of the pulp in the deckle. As a result, your mottled sheet will be quite a riot of color on one side with something near a write-able surface on the other side.

More examples of mottled surface sheets.

Adding Color in The Deckle

After a sheet's worth of pulp has been poured into the deckle of a pour hand mold you can throw in many other interesting components including other colored pulps, botanicals, glitter 'n glisten elements, pieces of cloth, etc. It's a whole world unto itself. Adding color at this point is easy and leads to all kinds of uniqueness in art and decoration.

Examples of color added in the deckle.

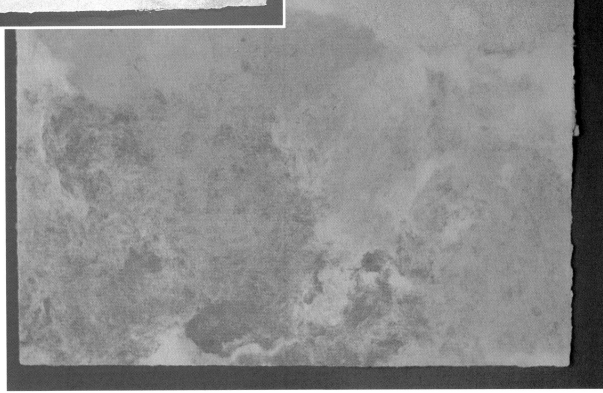

Example of color added in the deckle.

STEP 1. Prepare a sheet's worth of pulp. White is probably the best to show off the colors added later.

STEP 2. By recycling colored papers in a blender, prepare three colors of pulp. Put each in a cup and set aside.

STEP 3. Using pulp from Step 1, do the basic hand papermaking Steps 1 through 6.

STEP 4. Draw one of the colored pulps into a turkey baster. Using just a bit of gentle pressure on the baster's bulb, shoot some of the colored pulp into the white pulp at one corner of the deckle.

STEP 5. Repeat the action with each of the two other colored pulps in separate corners of the deckle.

STEP 6. Do the basic hand papermaking Steps 7 through 20.

ALTERNATIVE: This technique offers great room for exploration, experimentation, and a wide range of unique and wonderful papers. In Step 4 try holding the baster at different levels, with different amounts of pressure on the baster bulb, different thicknesses of colored pulp slurries in the baster, or put the baster end down into the pulp and shoot. Try different pulp guns (syrup dispenser, mustard container, etc.). Try anything your imagination can uncover as a way to enter colored pulps into the pulp already in the deckle. These sheets will likely be two-sided. Dispersion

Color(s) can be added gently or with force to the pulp in the deckle.

on one side of the sheet will be different than on the other because the colored pulp tends to sink. Close observation can lead to further manipulation of this phenomenon and how it works.

Adding Color While The Pulp Drains

Example of color added while the pulp drains.

As pulp drains in a pour hand mold deckle, colored pulp(s) can be added. The window of opportunity is brief. Does this result in any different effect than adding pulp before the mold is lifted? Yes, very subtly. Is it enough to warrant treatment as a separate technique? About all you can do is try it and decide for yourself.

There are rapid and slow draining pulps. For this technique, use a slow draining pulp. (See Hints and Helps, page 146, for more information on rapid and slow draining pulps.)

STEP 1. Prepare red and green pulp by recycling red and green papers. Put them in separate, easy to handle containers.
NOTE: Don't make the colored pulp slurries too thick or they will simply sink in a mass.

STEP 2. Prepare white pulp for a single sheet.
STEP 3. Do the basic hand papermaking Steps 1 through 6.
STEP 4. With one hand, lift the mold out of the water. With the other hand, immediately pour a small amount of red pulp into the draining pulp at one place in the deckle. Then quickly do the same with the green pulp at a different place in the deckle. Hold the mold level until drainage is complete.
NOTE: If you can't lift the mold with one hand, have someone else lift it so you can pour in the colored pulps.
STEP 5. Do the basic hand papermaking Steps 8 through 21.

Adding Color After The Sheet is Formed

Any slight change in the way color is added will change the final effect, subtly or dramatically. This is an area for exploration and exploitation and offers much discovery and fun.

STEP 1. By recycling colored papers, prepare three colored pulps (more or fewer if you wish). Put the pulp in separate containers for later use.

STEP 2. Prepare enough white pulp for a sheet.

STEP 3. Using the white pulp, form a sheet by doing the basic hand papermaking Steps 1 through 9.

STEP 4. Place the screen and new sheet on a drain rack in a tray or on some other flat surface.

STEP 5. Draw some colored pulp into a turkey baster.

NOTE: In the following steps, colored pulp will be added by two different techniques, "drop" and "dribble." Drop will be used on the new sheet's top half, dribble on the bottom half.

STEP 6. For the new sheet's top half, hold the baster vertically about 4″ above the sheet. Let pulp fall by gravity in single drops onto the wet surface, randomly or in a pattern. Repeat with the two other colored pulps.

NOTE: If the pulp is very diluted, it might tend to run out continuously. Place your finger over the baster opening to control this.

STEP 7. For the new sheet's bottom half, hold the baster almost horizontally about 2″ above the sheet. Moving the baster slowly, let pulp dribble out onto the new sheet's surface, using a little pressure on the baster bulb if necessary. Repeat with the two other colored pulps, dribbling them on top of, or immediately beside, preceding colors, or in entirely separate areas.

STEP 8. Complete making the sheet by doing basic hand papermaking Steps 10 through 12.

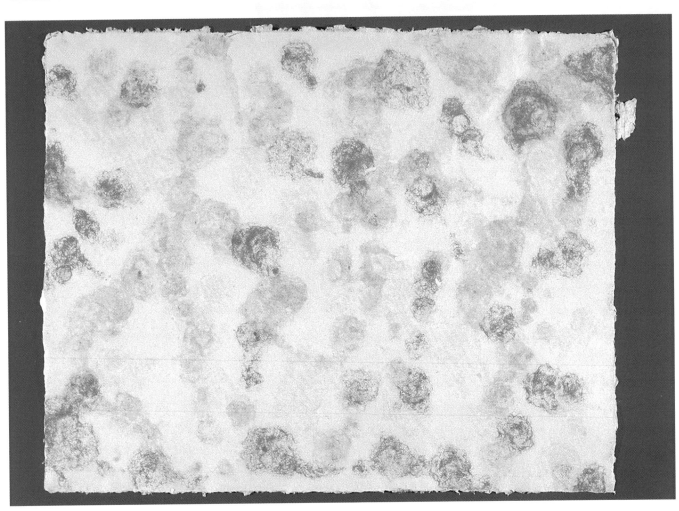

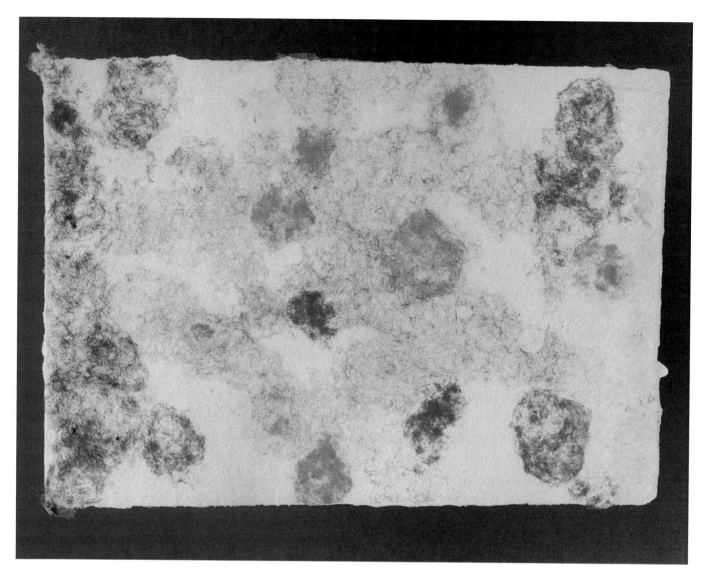

NOTE: In Steps 6 and 7, a whole range of effects can be obtained by varying (a) the thickness of the colored pulp slurry, (b) the distance of the baster above the sheet, and (c) the amount of pressure applied squeezing the baster bulb.

NOTE: When pulp is dropped on a new sheet's surface, it can create thinner areas in the sheet, affecting the new sheet's strength and uniformity. For decorative and artistic purposes, this is likely not serious.

ALTERNATIVE: Instead of doing Step 7 on page 58 directly on the new sheet's surface, do it on the surface of a piece of window screen (the cover screen in Greg Markim kits). Then pulp layer (see page 60) it onto the surface of the new sheet. A window screen surface provides more liberty in dropping and dribbling.

Pulp Layering

In the same way that one fiber bonds to another, a batch of fibers will bond to another batch. Because of this, one wet sheet can be laid on top of another, pressed, and dried to create a single thicker sheet (sheet layering).

Hence, pulp in all colors can be laid out in the form of an image on a second screen, then laid down on the surface of a newly formed wet sheet. This technique is often known as "pulp painting."

STEP 1. Do the basic hand papermaking Steps 1 through 9 and set aside the new sheet without removing any water.

STEP 2. Place a piece of window screen (cover screen in Greg Markim kits) on any type of drain rack.

STEP 3. Recycle two different colored papers into pulp. Put each color in a different container and set aside.

STEP 4. Draw some of one of the colored pulps into a pulp gun (turkey baster, mustard or catsup dispenser, etc.).

STEP 5. Place the pulp gun end over the middle at the top of the window screen. Dribble a continuous line of pulp down the screen's center to the bottom.

STEP 6. Repeat with the other colored pulp, dribbling across the screen (side-to-side) at the center. Now there is a line of colored pulp from top-to-bottom and a line of different colored pulp side-to-side, crossing in the middle.

STEP 7. Lift the window screen. Turn it upside-down so the pulp is on the bottom. Lower the window screen gently down onto the surface of the newly formed wet sheet made in Step 1. The two lines of colored pulp are now against and touching the surface of the new sheet.

STEP 8. Push a sponge down on top of the window screen to remove water.

STEP 9. Carefully peel the window screen off. The colored pulp will remain bonded to the first sheet.

NOTE: Window screen is coarse and some fibers might wrap around the screen's strands. When the screen is lifted these will cling, possibly lifting others too. Fibers are less likely to cling if the window screen is laid over a finer screen before the colored pulp is applied.

NOTE: See Sheet Layering on page 106 for layering an entire sheet on another.

STEP 10. Do the basic hand papermaking Steps 10 through 20.

NOTE: This technique is adaptable for specific images made with found patterns (cookie cutters, etc.), patterns cut out of food foam board or other material, or for colorful abstracts made by simply "blobbing" pulps onto the second screen with a variety of pulp guns.

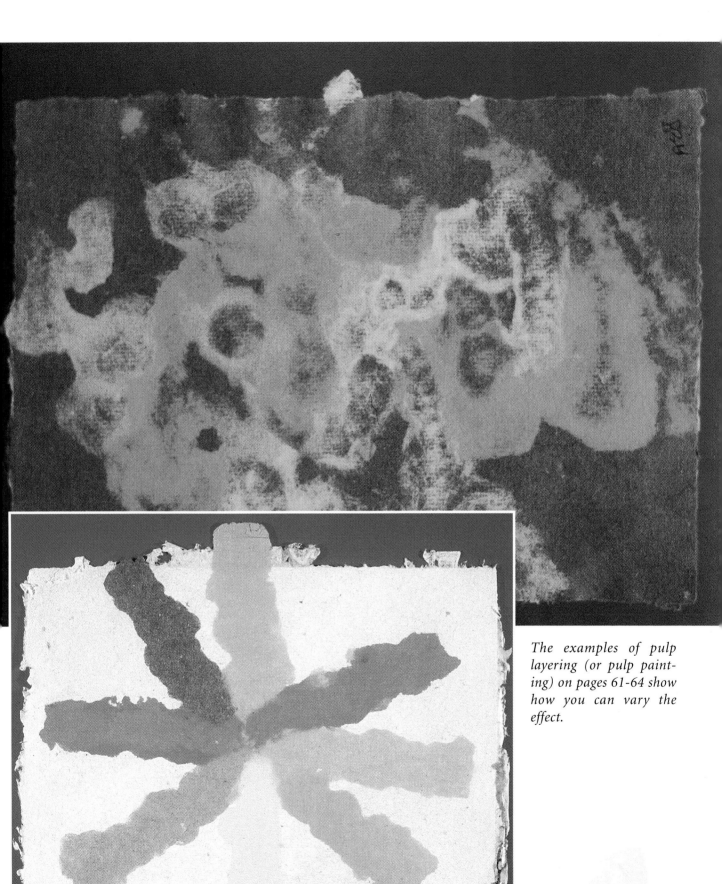

The examples of pulp layering (or pulp painting) on pages 61-64 show how you can vary the effect.

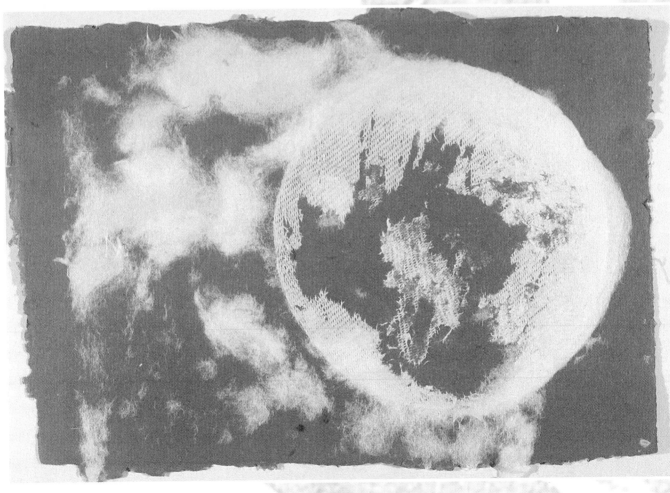

Pin Drawing

A pin can be used to "draw" with colored fibers on the surface of a newly formed wet sheet. When you dip a pin in pulp slurry, it will pick up fibers on its barrel. By lowering the pin horizontally to the wet sheet and dropping the point onto the surface, pin fibers and surface fibers will create a bond. If you pull the pin away, fibers will slide off the pin's barrel and be deposited onto the surface in a line. Thinness or thickness of the pulp slurry plays a large role in the line's nature.

The line of fibers can be manipulated after having been deposited. You can use the point of the pin to move it a bit to one side or the other and to straighten the line's edges. This is delicate and requires a careful touch. The point of the pin must engage colored fibers only.

Bend the pin just below its head (you don't want your fingertips to touch the sheet's surface).

Learn about thick and thin slurries (see Hints and Helps, page 146). Thick and thin slurries lay down different kinds of lines. See the difference by experimenting with thick, thin, and medium thick slurries. Experiment with thin wires. While I work with pins, there is room for discovery in trying thin wires. Bending a thin wire would be easier than bending a pin and pins tend to break rather than bend.

STEP 1. Do the basic hand papermaking Steps 1 through 10 but don't put on the cover screen.

STEP 2. Prepare a thick slurry of colored pulp and put part of it in a shallow container. Add water to the remainder to make a thin slurry and put it in another shallow container. Tall containers make it difficult to get the pin down into the pulp. Tipping the container to one side when dipping helps the pin to pick up fibers.

NOTE: For a first try, the following steps will take you through drawing a simple square, using the thick slurry for two sides and the thin slurry for the other two.

STEP 3. Draw a square on the new sheet's surface, starting with the vertical sides. Dip a pin into the thick slurry. Lift it out with pulp on its barrel. Lower the pin horizontally to the new sheet's surface until the fibers on the pin's barrel touch the sheet's surface. NOTE: Hold the pin at a bit of a slant so the fibers nearer the pin's end will touch the sheet's surface first.

STEP 4. Slowly slide the pin out of the pulp. Because the fibers touching the surface will have bonded slightly, the natural bond between the wet fibers on the pin will generally pull all or most of the pulp off the pin as it is withdrawn. By repeated dipping, make the line as long as you wish. Repeating, draw the square's other vertical side.

STEP 5. Dip the pin into the thinner pulp slurry and draw the square's two horizontal lines.

STEP 6. Put the cover screen over the new sheet and do the basic hand papermaking Steps 11 through 20.

STEP 7. Carefully examine and compare the nature of lines made by the thicker and thinner pulp slurries.

ALTERNATIVE: From the above simple project, move on to trying to make curved lines, laying several lines down adjacent to each other to make thicker lines, etc. Pin drawing can be a very sensitive medium for artistic expression.

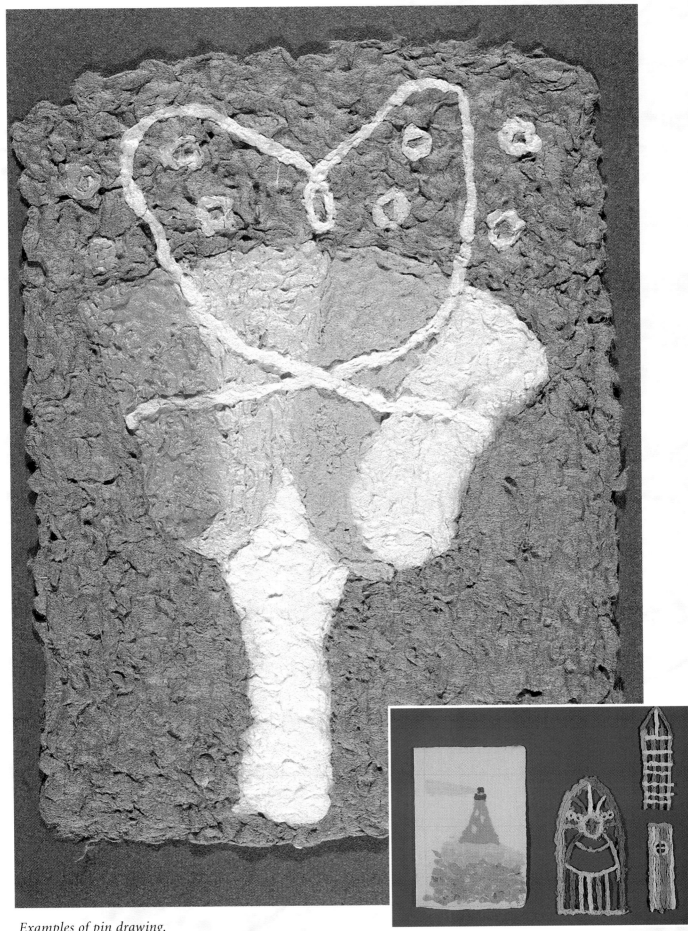

Examples of pin drawing.

Color by Small Opening Sprinkle

This technique doesn't produce a gross difference from some of the other techniques for adding color, but often it does provide a certain look of sufficient individuality to warrant its treatment as a separate technique.

This is another way to add color to the surface of a newly formed (wet) sheet. Colored pulps applied to a wet sheet's surface by being sprinkled from a pulp gun can provide a distinctive effect. One or more colors can be applied directly on the surface, as in the first project or by applying the color to a second screen and then pulp layering it (see page 60) onto the new sheet as in the second project.

Sprinkling here means dispensing thin (diluted) pulps through a small opening in some type of pulp gun by using a salt-shaker action.

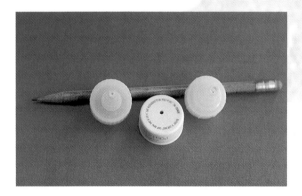

The small openings are in caps or spouts of screw-on caps of containers such as plastic soda bottles, or lotion or ointment containers, etc.

Container caps (for soda bottles, etc.) without holes can be drilled with a 7/64″ drill or punctured with a 6d nail.

One problem that might occur is continual plugging of the small opening. Combat this by running pulp in the blender until there are absolutely no chunks remaining or by keeping the pulp slurry in the container thin. Small openings can be unplugged with a pin or toothpick. Experiment with larger or smaller openings.

Example 1

STEP 1. Make two colored pulps by recycling colored papers in a blender. Run until no chunks are present.

STEP 2. Put a very thin colored pulp into a container with a small opening.

STEP 3. Prepare some white pulp and form a sheet by

doing the basic hand papermaking Steps 1 through 10, but in Step 10 don't put the cover screen over the new sheet.

STEP 4. Put a finger over the small opening in the container of colored pulp and shake the container vigorously to disperse the fibers inside. Turn the container upside-down and shake the container to deposit color on the wet sheet's surface.

STEP 5. Repeat Step 4 with the second colored pulp.

STEP 6. Put the cover screen over the new sheet. Do the basic hand papermaking Steps 11 through 21.

Example 2

STEP 1. Do Steps 1 through 3 above.

STEP 2. Put a second screen on a drain rack.

STEP 3. Sprinkle pulp from the small-opening container onto the screen.

STEP 4. Lift the screen. While holding it, turn it upside-down so the colored pulp is on the bottom.

STEP 5. Gently lower the screen, putting the colored pulp on the bottom on the wet surface of the new sheet.

STEP 6. Do the basic hand papermaking Steps 11 through 21.

NOTE: Getting pulp to come out when the small-opening container is being shaken will vary widely. Very thin pulp might run out. Control the flow by putting your finger over the opening if droplets are desired. Less diluted pulp might require various degrees of shaking.

Veining

Veining can be a technique for specialization. Effects can be very dramatic. Propelling a thin stream of diluted pulp into a delicate newly formed sheet has all kinds of visual implications. It can also raise great physical havoc with the sheet.

This falls somewhere in the delicate area between achieving visual effect and preserving the physical integrity of the sheet. The veined effect is always satisfying.

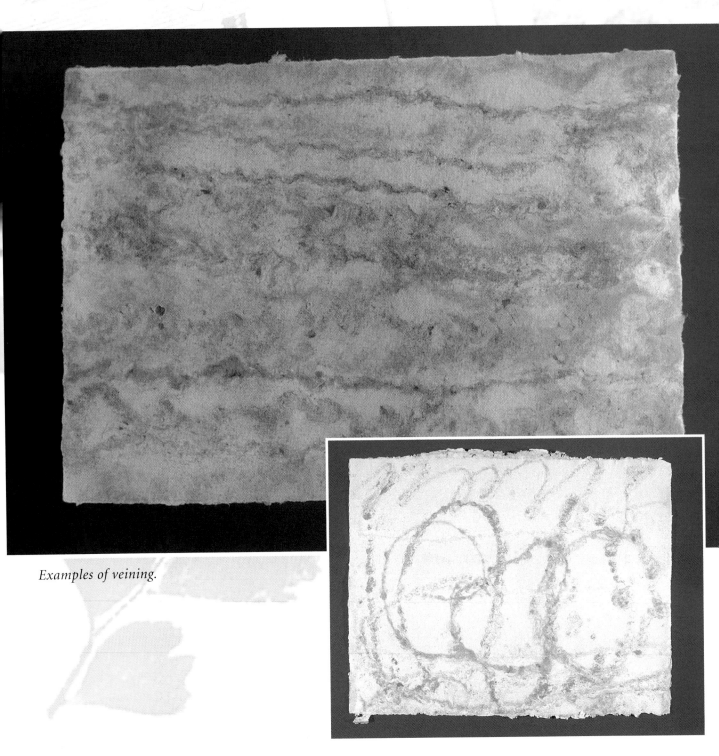

Examples of veining.

STEP 1. Select a pulp gun with a very small opening in the cap or spout.

STEP 2. Prepare two pulps of different colors. Draw a thin slurry of one of the colored pulps into the pulp gun.

STEP 3. Form a white sheet by doing the basic hand papermaking Steps 1 through 9.

STEP 4. After removing the deckle, place the screen and new sheet on a drain rack in a drain pan or on another surface as in the basic hand papermaking Step 10, but don't apply the cover screen.

STEP 5. Shake the pulp gun. With some force, squirt a steady, thin stream across the surface of the new sheet.

NOTE: The pulp stream hitting the new sheet will displace fibers. Colored fibers will be left where the stream hits. Whether the colored fibers replace the displaced fibers, preventing a void in the sheet, depends on the consistency of the pulp slurry in the gun, how much force is applied to the squirt, the angle at which the pulp stream is aimed at the sheet surface, and how rapidly the pulp stream is moved across the new sheet's surface (if not rapid enough, the pulp stream will literally dig a hole). Consider and work with these variables.

NOTE: Starting the pulp stream somewhere on the sheet can produce an unattractive effect where the pulp stream first hits. Try starting the pulp stream at a point just off, but right beside, the sheet, then move it across the sheet's surface. The pulp stream can be moved in a straight, zigzag, circular, or any other line, across the sheet's surface.

STEP 6. Repeat Step 5 with the second color of pulp.

STEP 7. Do the basic hand papermaking Steps 10 through 20.

NOTE: The shooting stream of pulp can seriously tear up the newly formed sheet and still leave a highly dramatic, desirable visual effect. In this case, couch the veined new sheet off the screen onto a couch material. Then make a second sheet on a piece of window screen. Pulp layer (see page 60) it onto the back of the veined sheet. Choosing the right color for the second sheet (which will show through the voids in the veined sheet) can further enhance the veined sheet's visual impact.

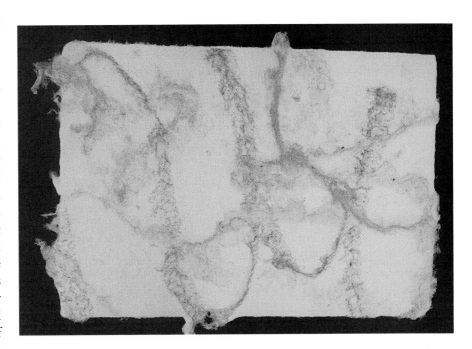

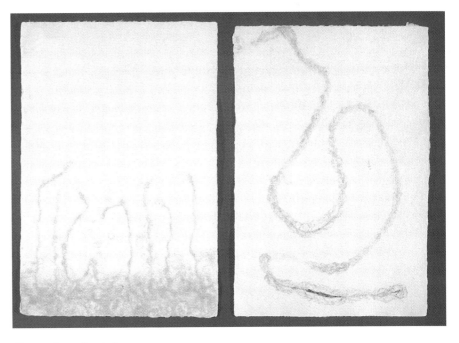

Examples of veining.

Adding Color on a Muddy Surface

This technique is a very specialized area. It is only subtly different than adding color after the sheet is formed. Yet, to the sensitive eye or creative spirit, the difference is definite.

Use of the word "muddy" is definitive. Some papers are heavily coated with clay or contain other non-fiber materials. When recycled, these papers make a pulp that leans toward muddy.

Clay coated and calendered papers can be identified by a shiny surface. But papers that are only machine glazed are also shiny. When choosing papers for this technique, try to find the shiniest paper. The surface of a newly made sheet formed with muddy pulp seems to have a maximum vulnerability. It will respond uniquely to liquid dropped on it. Consequently, this technique will have a definite niche in the resource bin of ardent practitioners of decorative and art papers.

This technique has much in common with adding color after a sheet is formed, but for those papermakers who might find it engrossing, we offer it here as its own project.

STEP 1. Recycle some white paper with the shiniest surface you can find. Slick magazines are usually printed on paper needed for this project. Blend enough paper to make a sheet a bit thicker than average.

NOTE: If there is not considerable foam during blending, the paper might not be coated.

STEP 2. From non-shiny paper, prepare two colors of pulp and put each in a separate container. (More colors can be used if desired.)

STEP 3. Do the basic hand papermaking Steps 1 through 9.

STEP 4. Draw some of one of the colored pulps into a pulp gun.

STEP 5. Holding the pulp gun 6″ to 10″ above the new sheet, drop single drops onto the new sheet's muddy surface.

STEP 6. Repeat Steps 4 and 5 with the other colored pulp(s).

STEP 7. Do the basic hand papermaking Steps 10 through 21.

NOTE: The consistency of the pulp slurry dropped dictates the effect produced. A slurry just thick enough to register color on the sheet's surface will likely be thin enough to feather and fuse into the adjacent sheet surface area. Drops from a too-thick slurry will tend to sit as lumps. The subtle blending of thinner slurries into the sheet surface is the unique hallmark effect of this technique.

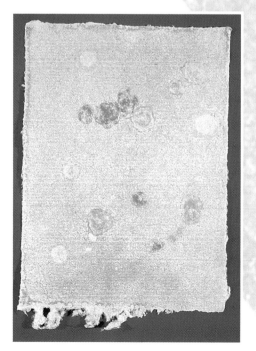

Examples of color added on a muddy surface.

Puddling

Puddling is fun exploration and discovery. It can be very dramatic and artistically productive. Above all, each of its creations will certainly be unique.

Probably the real key to this technique is Step 3. Concentrate on it. All in all, working with this technique can provide rich rewards and some striking art.

Examples of puddling.

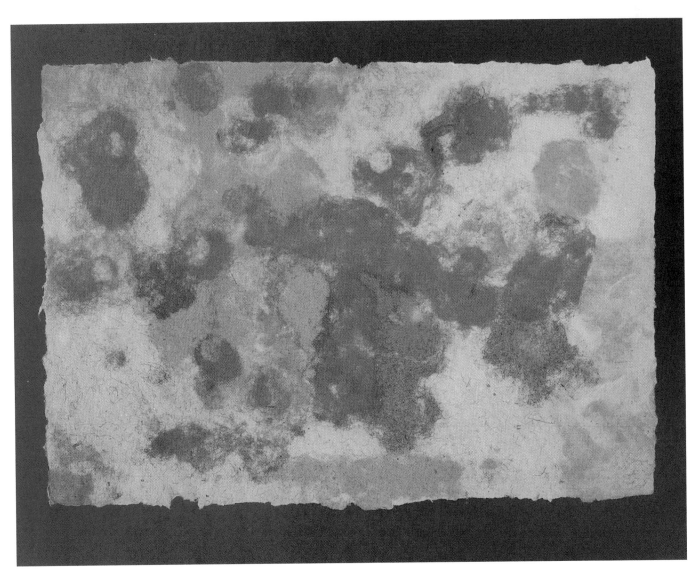

STEP 1. Prepare pulps of four different colors. (More or fewer colors will work. Four is simply a good starting point.)

STEP 2. Do the basic hand papermaking Steps 1 through 3.

STEP 3. Lower the hand mold into the water until the screen is barely beneath the surface. Keep the screen as steady as possible at its level beneath the water's surface.

NOTE: Very little water must be above the screen. There must be enough to allow some mobility of the pulp but not so much that the pulp can scatter. Experiment.

STEP 4. With a pulp gun, drop colored pulp at a specific place over the screen. The pulp should form a puddle. If it spreads and separates, the pulp is either too thin or has been applied with too much force or the screen might be too far under the water. Try using a thicker pulp, dropping it from a lower height, or moving the screen closer to the water's surface.

STEP 5. Repeat Step 4 with the other colored pulps at different places over the screen, until the entire screen is covered. You might find this a bit tricky, but it can be done. Make sure there are no small voids in the pulp over the screen's surface. This can take close examination. Eliminating voids can be tricky because of the way the various pulps move. If nothing else works, lift the mold out of the water and fill the voids with a suitably thick pulp from the pulp gun. Or with a little more water above the surface, try to distribute the pulp with your fingers or other stirring device. Don't over-mix. Some voids might not be bad. Should voids persist, form a quite thin sheet of an appropriate color on a second screen and sheet layer it (see page 106) onto the puddled sheet. The second sheet's color showing through the puddled sheet's voids can be quite effective.

STEP 6. Do the basic hand papermaking Steps 7 through 20.

Examples of puddling.

Bordering/ Self-Framing

To put a border on one edge or entirely around a sheet or to self-frame a sheet, use this technique, an adaptation of adding color after a sheet is formed.

Application of color can be made directly to the wet sheet in the deckle or indirectly by pulp layering (page 60).

Each is shown in a project.

Direct Application

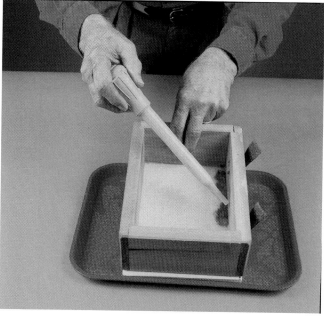

Keep the point of the baster near the deckle wall and release pulp very gently.

STEP 1. Prepare enough pulp for one sheet. Prepare several colors of pulp for adding as the border or frame.

STEP 2. Do the basic hand papermaking Steps 1 through 8 but don't loosen the straps.

STEP 3. If you want just one edge bordered, do this step along one edge. If you want the entire sheet bordered or self-framed, do this step along all edges. Draw a colored pulp into a pulp gun. Drop/dribble the colored pulp on the edge of the sheet next to the deckle, along one or all edges. Repeat with as many colored pulps as you wish.

NOTE: The amount of pulp you apply as a border or self-frame depends on your taste. Applying pulp sparingly will keep sheet edges more uniformly thick with the sheet's center. For a self-frame, more pulp might give more of a sense of a frame.

STEP 4. Pull the mold's straps loose. Do the basic hand papermaking Steps 9 through 20.

Indirect Application

STEP 1. Do Step 1 above.

STEP 2. Do the basic hand papermaking Steps 1 through 10, but don't put the cover screen over the new sheet.

STEP 3. Put the cover screen (or a similar piece of window screen) on any kind of a drain rack. Put the deckle on top of the window screen.

STEP 4. Do Step 3 of the direct application project, dropping the colored pulp(s) on the window screen (just as on the new sheet).

STEP 5. Remove the deckle, then lift the window screen. Continuing to hold it, turn it over so the pulp is on the bottom.

STEP 6. Carefully matching the outside edges of the pulp to the outside edges of the new sheet, lower the window screen, dropping the colored pulp onto the new sheet.

STEP 7. Apply a sponge to the window screen to remove water. After removing as much water as possible, carefully lift the window screen. The colored pulps will remain on the edge(s) of the new sheet.

NOTE: Coarser screens can be notorious for not releasing all of the pulps put on them. See page 134.

STEP 8. Do the basic hand papermaking Steps 13 through 20.

Edge Dipping

If you dip the edge of a pour hand mold screen into water, you have a pool into which you can pour colored pulps, glitter, etc., and then pulp layer it onto a newly formed wet sheet. The width and length of the pool is your decision. This technique offers great variety in decorative and artistic expression.

STEP 1. Prepare three different colors of pulp.

STEP 2. Do the basic hand papermaking Steps 1 through 10, but don't put the cover screen over the newly formed sheet.

STEP 3. Put a second screen into the hand mold, as in the basic hand papermaking Steps 1 through 3.

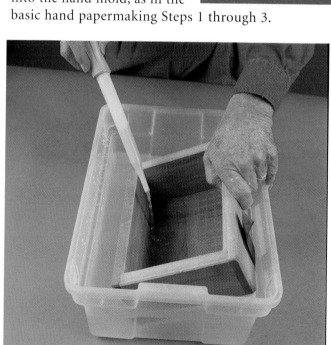

The tilted hand mold permits water only near the edge of the screen. Pulp can go only where the water is.

STEP 4. Dip the hand mold at a slanted angle into the vat. Water will come up over the papermaking screen's edge. Keep the mold at a steep angle so that quite deep water covers about 1/4 the screen.

Here, "edge dippings" have been pulp layered onto a sheet. Edge dippings can be recognized by a straight edge on one side and ragged edge on the other. More than one edge dipping can be applied to a single sheet.

STEP 5. Hold the mold steady. Into the pool of water above the screen, pour different colored pulps in different places. Don't pour in too much pulp. Add glitter if desired.

STEP 6. Lift the mold out of the water. For the first effort, lift it straight up, not changing the angle. In later efforts, lift the mold out with a bit of a scooping action. This will cause water and some pulp to wash a little higher on the screen as the mold is lifted. This can result in a ragged edge as the pulp lands on the screen.

STEP 7. Pulp layer (see page 60) the pulp on the screen onto the newly formed sheet.

STEP 8. Do the basic hand papermaking Steps 10 through 20.

*Examples of
edge dipping.*

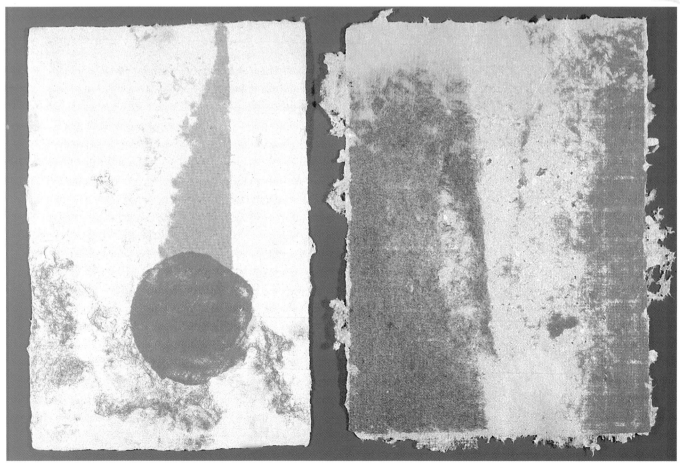

Botanicals Added In the Blender

Botanicals are things that grow, or parts thereof. Examples are flowers, their petals and leaves, tree leaves, grasses, corn stalk pith, ferns, arbor vita, etc. Fine ferns and delicate flower blossoms and petals seem to be favorites. For pressure drying, quite bulky items can be used. For heat drying by iron, hard, bulky items generally cannot be handled.

Added in the blender, botanicals shred. The length of blender time determines the degree of shredding, all the way to pulverizing. Experiment with blender time.

NOTE: Many non-botanical materials also will shred or pulverize and can be used in the same way as botanicals.

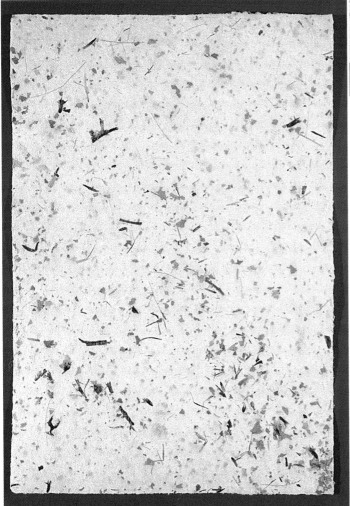

STEP 1. Put new pulp or paper to be recycled in the blender with water.

STEP 2. Select one or several botanicals to be added to the new sheet (do not overload the first time). Put half in the blender.

STEP 3. Run the blender 13 seconds.

STEP 4. Add the other half of the botanicals. Run the blender two more seconds.

NOTE: Running botanicals for two different time lengths in the same batch of pulp will show the different effects side-by-side in the same sheet.

STEP 5. Do the basic hand papermaking Steps 1 through 20. Note the difference between the longer and shorter blender-run botanicals. If your sheet is wall-to-wall botanicals, try a sheet adding very few botanicals.

Botanicals Added In the Deckle: Internal Embedment

Adding botanicals in the deckle can make a sheet very different from one made by adding them in the blender. It might be interesting to use the same type of botanicals you used in the blender.

NOTE: Any non-botanical materials not too bulky, such as bits of fabric, ribbons, threads, etc., can be used as well as or with botanicals.

Examples of internal embedment.

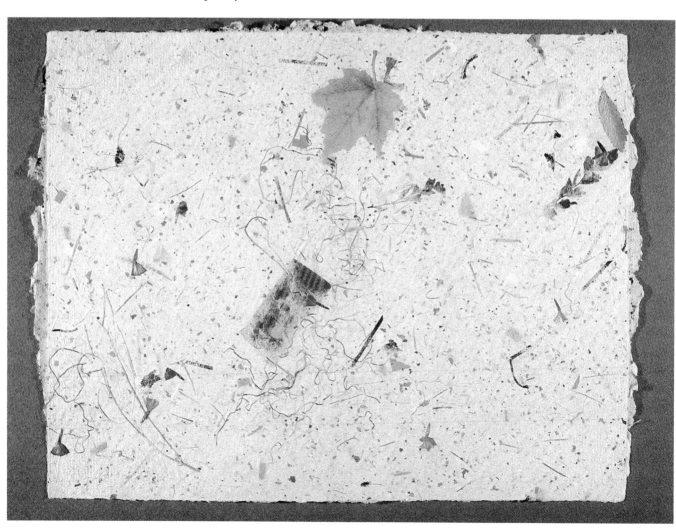

STEP 1. Assemble whatever botanicals you want to add to your handmade sheet. Break them into pieces the size you want to appear on the sheet.

STEP 2. Do the basic hand papermaking Steps 1 through 6.

STEP 3. Add the botanical pieces to the pulp in the deckle. Botanicals will likely float on top of the pulp. Should they continue to float through Step 5, they will not become a part of the new sheet but will simply be lying on the sheet's surface. Consequently, something needs to be done to get at least a few fibers over them to tie them into the sheet. The next steps will help.

STEP 4. Push the botanicals down into the pulp. Hopefully, when they rise again, they will have a few fibers over them. If some of the botanicals stay buried, gently urge them toward the surface.

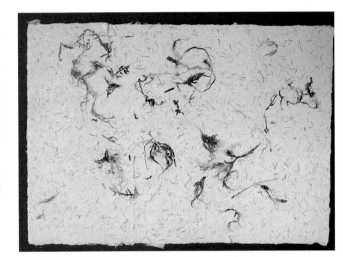

STEP 5. Lift the hand mold out of the water. Watch the botanicals as the pulp drains. If some are still floating when most of the pulp is down on the screen, try pushing them down a bit into the pulp as the last fibers settle. To do this, hold the mold with one hand or immediately after the mold is out of the water, set it on a level surface.

STEP 6. Do the basic hand papermaking Steps 8 through 20.

NOTE: To place botanicals at a specific place on a sheet's surface, see the next technique, Surface Embedment.

Examples of internal embedment.

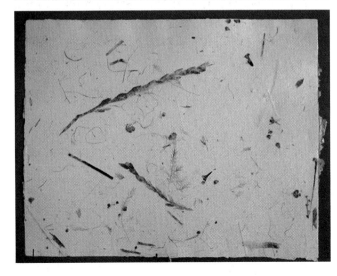

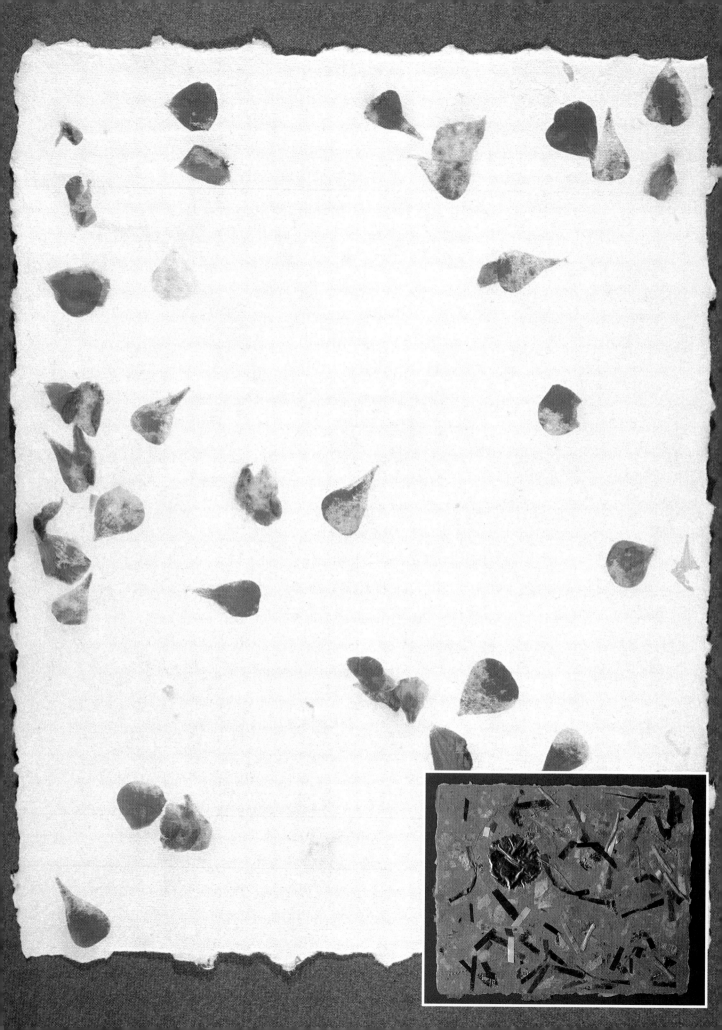

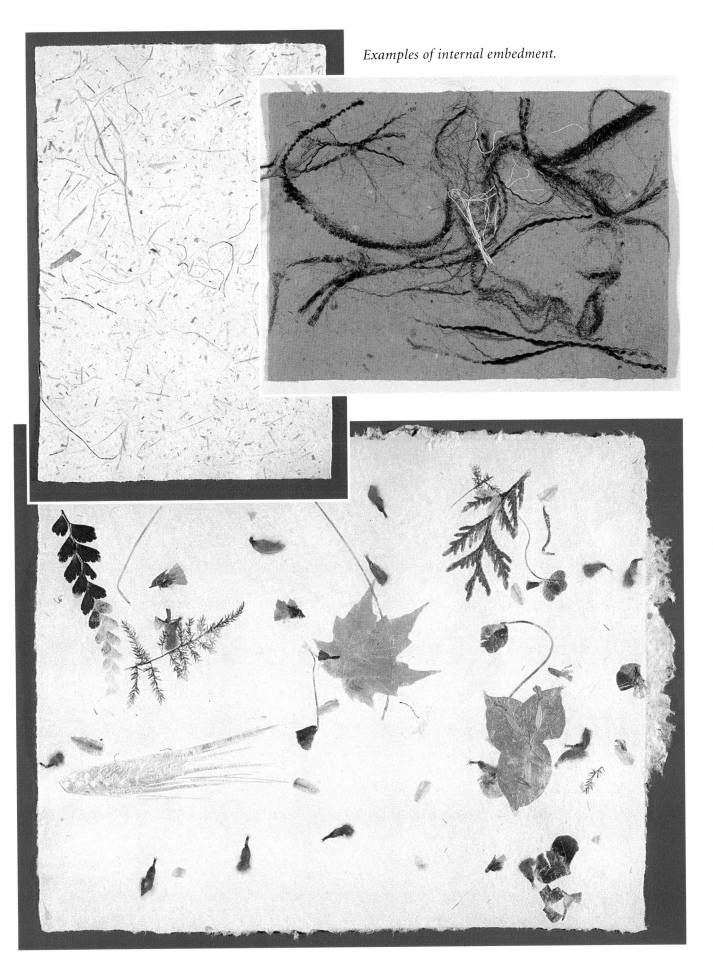

Examples of internal embedment.

Surface Embedment

Botanicals are excellent for this technique. Many other flat items that are not too bulky can be embedded on a paper's surface. If paper is dried under pressure, most any suitable botanical or non-botanical can be used. If paper is dried by heat, bulky unyielding botanicals or non-botanicals will be disturbed by the iron, generally making a hole in the sheet. A few experiments will show you what works and what doesn't.

Some items that can be embedded are fall leaves, ferns, grass, and other botanicals; bits of fabric, threads, ribbons; photos, newspaper and magazine cutouts (pictures, illustrations, comics, photos of news makers and sports and other celebrities, friends, etc.); shaped pieces of shiny foil or illustrations from Christmas cards; anything that strikes your fancy.

Embedment of botanicals and other materials can be done in two ways—with and without a pulp gun.

Examples of surface embedment.

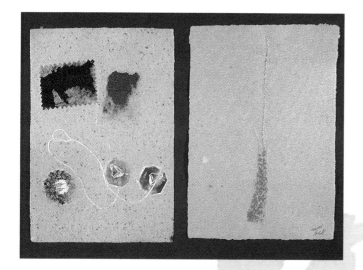

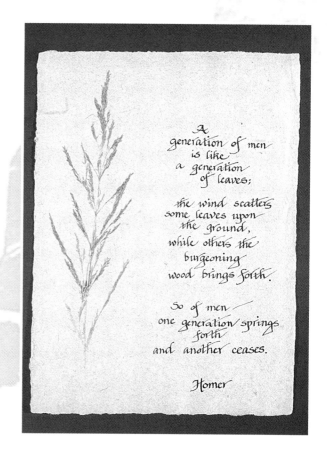

Examples of surface embedment.

Surface Embedment

STEP 1. Select a botanical or non-botanical to embed.

STEP 2. Do the basic hand papermaking Steps 1 through 6.

STEP 3. Dip the embedding item in the pulp in the deckle, then remove it.

STEP 4. Hold the embedding item in one hand and lift the mold from the vat with your other hand. If you can't lift the mold with one hand, get a friend to help or lift the mold quickly out of the water, set it on a level surface, then place the embedding item.

STEP 5. Watch the progress of drainage closely. When 1/2 to 3/4 of the pulp has drained, place the embedding item down firmly on the fibers already on the screen. The rest of the pulp will drain, embedding the item and making it an integral part of the sheet.

NOTE: There are fast-draining and slow-draining pulps (see Hints and Helps, page 146). A slow-draining pulp should be used here.

STEP 6. Do the basic hand papermaking Steps 8 through 20. The truly successful embedment is one where the item doesn't pop up from the dried sheet's surface when the sheet is flexed.

NOTE: Heat drying with an iron is always tricky with any surface embedment. It's always preferable to dry the sheet slowly under pressure.

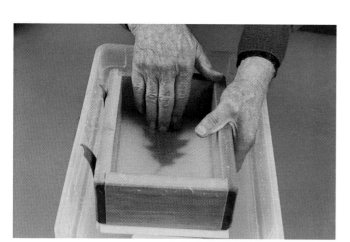

Pushing the leaf down onto the fibers already on the screen.

The remaining fibers descend, pinning the leaf to the surface of the sheet.

Surface Embedment with a Pulp Gun

STEP 1. Select the botanical or non-botanical item to be embedded.

STEP 2. Prepare pulp. Pour a small amount into a container for later use. Use the rest to make a sheet.

STEP 3. Do the basic hand papermaking Steps 1 through 6.

STEP 4. Dip the embedding item in the pulp in the deckle, then lay it aside.

STEP 5. Do the basic hand papermaking Steps 7 through 9.

STEP 6. Lay the embedding item in position on the surface of the sheet.

STEP 7. Add just a bit of water to the container of pulp saved in Step 2. Draw some of it into a pulp gun.

STEP 8. Carefully dribble pulp along the edges of the embedding item.

NOTE: The consistency of the pulp in the pulp gun and the amount you dribble on the embedded item are decided pretty much by experience. Too little won't embed the item and too much will bury it. Watch closely to see what's happening as pulp is dribbled.

STEP 9. Do the basic hand papermaking Steps 10 through 20. Dry the sheet under pressure, not with heat. (Heat drying can be done only if the embedded item is very flat and does not rise above the sheet's surface.)

Embossing

A good subject for spirited debate at a coffee conversation would be, "Where does texturing end and embossing begin?"

Embossing is raising or lowering in a conscious pattern, part(s) of a paper (or other) surface in relation to what would be considered the paper's normal surface. It might be referred to as exaggerated texturing. (See Texturing, page 98.)

Embossing does indeed add a dimension to paper. It can lend a particular paper item a very commanding desirable air.

Embossing is often done to paper after the paper is manufactured. Here is a way to do it as the paper is made.

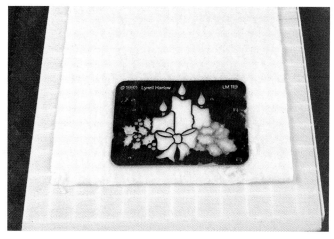

An embossing plate pressed down on the surface of a wet sheet.

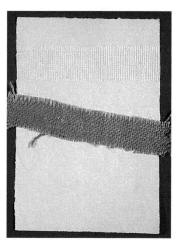

At top, a fall leaf left a colored as well as an embossed image. At bottom, a coarse cloth such as burlap, can make an embossed strip.

An embossed sheet lies on top of the embossed felt on which it was made.

STEP 1. Select a rough or patterned surface with which you want to emboss a sheet of paper. Craft stores offer a great number of metal embossing plates. They also offer an immense choice of plastic stencils, many of which can be used for embossing handmade paper as it is being made. Look at small, reasonably flat jewelry.

STEP 2. Prepare pulp and do the basic hand papermaking Steps 1 through 10, but don't put the cover screen over the new sheet.

STEP 3. Place the embossing plate or surface on the surface of the newly formed wet sheet. Carefully press down on the plate, observing the new sheet's pulp rise into the embossing plate's open areas. If you're using jewelry or other surface, the embossing surface is put down directly on the sheet's surface. The jewelry or other piece must be sufficiently flat and thin to be compatible with the remaining steps of this project.

STEP 4. Put the cover screen over the new sheet and embossing piece.

STEP 5. Leaving the embossing piece in place, do the basic hand papermaking Steps 11 through 17.

STEP 6. Replace the top and bottom wet couch sheets with dry ones. With the embossing piece still in place, put the new sheet and couch sheets under pressure in a press or under weight of some kind.

NOTE: Leaving the embossing piece in place through the papermaking steps means the sheet must be handled very carefully. Any shifting of the embossing piece will distort the embossing.

STEP 7. Change couch sheets (or other absorbent materials) as they get damp until the sheet is dry.

NOTE: If using small flat jewelry or other embossing surface that's smaller than the sheet, handle it in the same manner as an embossing plate. Place it on the wet sheet's surface and leave it there all the way through drying.

STEP 8. Carefully remove the dry sheet, then remove the embossing piece. This should result in an excellently embossed sheet.

NOTE: When embossing, it's best to dry the sheet over time under the pressure of a stack of books or in a press, with the paper between absorbent materials.

ALTERNATIVE: Whole surfaces of sheets can be embossed by simply following the Board Drying technique (page 100), using the embossing surface as the surface upon which the sheet is dried. Or, there are embossed felts at most craft stores. Instead of a cover screen, put an embossed felt over the new sheet in basic hand papermaking Step 11. Leave it on the sheet through final drying.

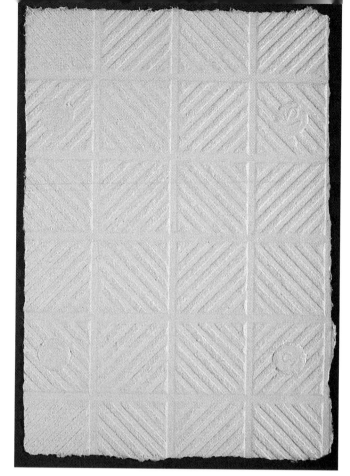

Sheets embossed by the back of ceramic tiles.

At left, an embossment from a ceramic tile. At right, a heart card (double deckle) embossed by a heart form found at a craft store.

Small jewelry can be used as an embossing plate.

At left, an embossed sheet. At right, the same embossment in another sheet along with the embossing plate used for both.

Deckle Division

Deckle division is simply dividing your hand mold's deckle into two or more compartments. In an undivided deckle, you can pour only one kind or color of pulp. In a deckle divided into two separate compartments, you can pour in two kinds or colors of pulp—one in each compartment. If you remove the divider while the two pulps are draining (after the mold is lifted from the water), the two pulps will flow into each other. This can produce dramatic effects. It results in a single sheet made of two different pulps.

Examples of sheets made using divided deckles.

STEP 1. Cut a straight edge along one of the long sides of a piece of food foam board (the kind meat or pastries are packaged on) that is longer than the deckle of your hand mold is wide.

STEP 2. At the middle of the mold, put the straight edge of the board across the top of the mold, from long side to long side.

STEP 3. With a pen or pencil, mark the foam board exactly at the inside of the deckle wall on both sides.

STEP 4. With scissors or a knife, cut the foam board straight up from each point marked in Step 3. This should result in a piece of foam board that will slide down inside the deckle between the long sides, dividing the deckle into two compartments. The divider should fit tightly enough to securely stay in place by friction. If not, cut another foam board piece a bit wider. Though a bit tricky, it can be done.

STEP 5. Prepare the deckle. Slide the deckle divider (foam board) into the deckle at roughly the deckle's midpoint.

STEP 6. Place the deckle into the vat.

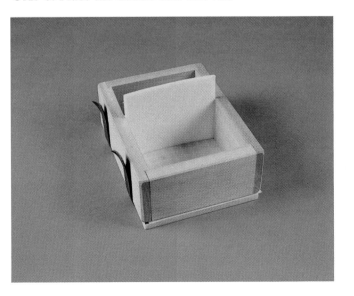

STEP 7. Prepare 3/4 of a sheet's worth of white pulp and 3/4 of a sheet's worth of colored pulp.

STEP 8. Gently pour the white pulp into one half of the deckle. Pour the colored pulp into the other half.

STEP 9. Agitate the pulp gently in both compartments.

STEP 10. With one hand, lift the mold up and out of the water.

STEP 11. Watch the pulp drainage. When 1/4 to 1/2 of the deckle's pulp has drained, pull the foam divider quickly straight up and out. The portions of the pulps not drained will flow into each other, forming a single sheet. Pulps can sometimes be made to flow into each other more forcefully by gently rocking the mold after the divider has been lifted. This can create more dramatic sheets. Experiment.

NOTE: If you are unable to lift the hand mold with one hand, get someone to help, or lift the mold and set it quickly on a surface, then lift the divider.

STEP 12. Do the basic hand papermaking Steps 8 through 20.

NOTE: This technique will produce a two-sided sheet. On one side, the line where the two pulps meet will be indistinct or almost nonexistent. On the other, it will likely be sharply defined.

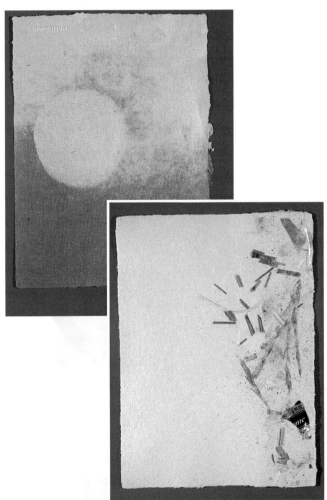

Examples of sheets made using divided deckles.

The effect you can produce with multiple dividers. The sheet on the right shows added pulp layering.

On one side of the sheet there's a sharp dividing line as shown above. On the other side, the pulps flow together to varying degrees as shown below.

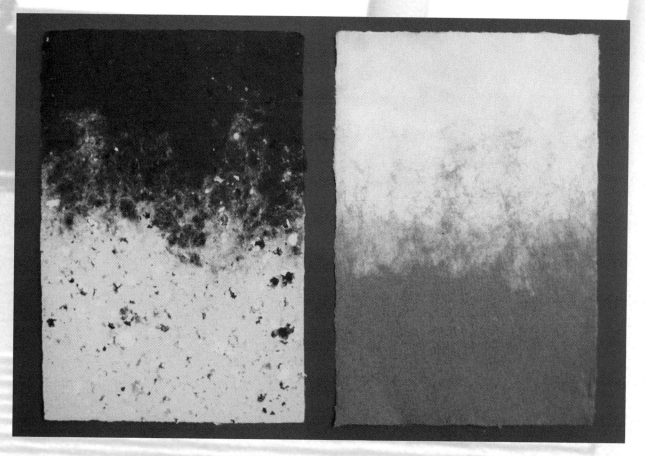

Screen Block Out: Windows

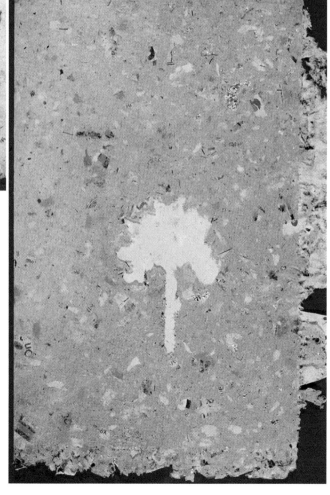

Here's a papermaking truism: "Where the water goes, the fiber goes." Consequently, if you block off part of your screen's surface, the water won't go there and neither will the fibers.

If you want to make a sheet half the size of your hand mold, simply cover half your screen with a solid material. No water or fibers will go there. So it follows that if you put some solid material cut in the shape of a heart on the middle of your screen, fibers would land everywhere on the screen except where the heart is. Your sheet would have a heart-shaped hole, or window, in it. This means you can have a window in your sheet in any shape you can cut out of some solid material such as wood, plastic, etc. Just cut it out, lay it on your screen, and make a sheet of paper. It's another world to explore.

Examples of windows in sheets.

STEP 1. Cut an image out of some flat, solid material such as a foam food tray or a thin board. Cut something easy first like a heart, square, or other simple shape. The size must be smaller than the papermaking screen.

A heart window lies in place on the screen in a newly formed sheet.

STEP 2. Prepare pulp and do the basic hand papermaking Steps 1 through 4.

STEP 3. Place the cutout image from Step 1 down on the screen wherever you wish. Hold it down firmly so no pulp runs under it.

STEP 4. With your other hand, pour the pulp into the deckle. If this gets too difficult, ask someone to help you, especially in the next step.

STEP 5. Keeping the image firmly on the screen, lift the hand mold out of the water. Hold it level while the water drains.

STEP 6. Do the basic hand papermaking Steps 8 through 10, but don't put the cover screen over the new sheet.

STEP 7. With great care, lift the image from the screen. Watch the pulp around the edges of the image so that it doesn't rise with the image. Let water drain for several minutes before lifting the image. If you used foam board, you can insert a pin at a slant into the image to help lift it.

STEP 8. Put a cover screen over the new sheet and do the basic hand papermaking Steps 11 through 20.

ALTERNATIVE: Combine screen block out with pulp layering (page 60). This can put a mottled surface sheet on the back of a plain sheet, with the colorful mottled surface showing through the void. Or think in terms of greeting cards. A heart-shaped void on the card's front will show the art or words that are on the card's inside.

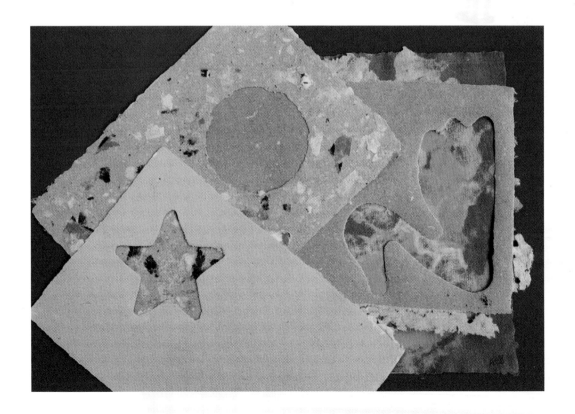

Texturing

Wet surfaces of newly formed sheets are easily textured. The wetter the better. The tiny fibers are to a degree cushioned in water. Any textured surface put down on them will, in a sense, float the fibers to positions matching the surface put down upon them.

This opens more worlds than one mind can conquer. Think about all the cloth surfaces in a large fabric store. Each can be used to texture a newly formed sheet of paper. Add to these all other flat surfaces in the world. Each can be put on paper. As you move through the world, keep your eye out for textures on surfaces. Wander through fabric stores, but also be aware of non-fabric surfaces.

In the following projects, try a texture that is subtle, then one that is more obvious.

(Above) Texturing can be found in many places including the inside of a light bulb carton.

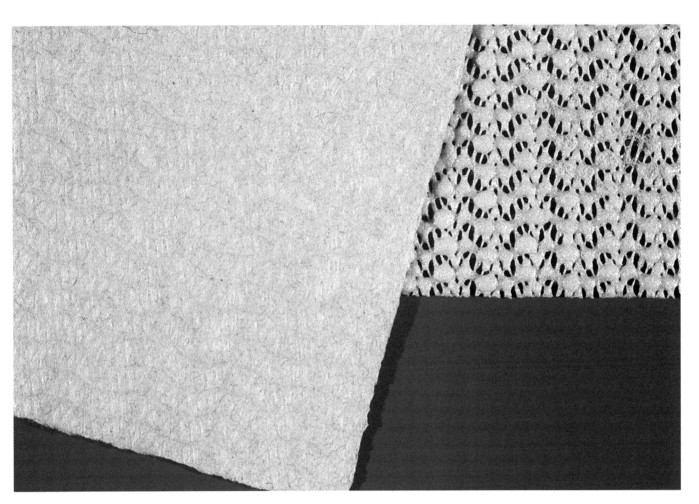

Example of textured sheets.

Fine Texture

STEP 1. Choose a piece of cloth with a very fine weave, such as bed sheeting. If it's a large piece, cut a piece close to the size of the paper sheet you're texturing.

STEP 2. Do the basic hand papermaking Steps 1 through 10 but don't put on the cover screen.

STEP 3. Lay the piece of bed sheeting over the new paper sheet. Leave it on the sheet through all remaining steps.

STEP 4. Do the basic hand papermaking Steps 11 through 20, *leaving the piece of bed sheet on the paper sheet.*

STEP 5. After the paper sheet dries, carefully remove the piece of bed sheet. Closely examine the paper sheet's surface. Then move your fingertips across it to feel the texture.

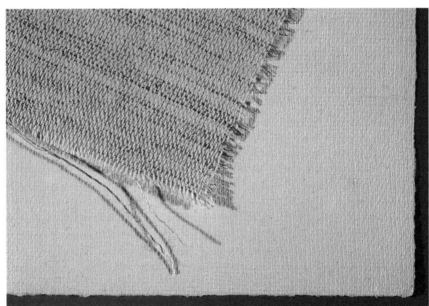

Coarse Texture

STEP 1. Choose a piece of cloth with a pronounced, rough, dimensional surface. Perhaps you can find cloth that is ribbed. Cut a piece close to the size of the paper sheet you're texturing.

STEP 2. Repeat Steps 2 through 5 above.

Board Drying

Board drying is a very old technique. It was practiced by early Chinese papermakers who built ovens with smooth stucco sides upon which they couched new wet handmade sheets. No couching material was kept over the sheets. A fire inside the oven aided drying.

The surface used in this technique need not be a board. It can be any water-safe surface that appeals to you.

Old Chinese board drying system. (Courtesy of the Robert C. Williams American Museum of Papermaking, featuring the Dard Hunter Collection.)

Examples of board dried sheets.

Example of a board dried sheet.

STEP 1. Select a board or other flat surface at least 2″ longer and wider than the paper sheet you're making. Be sure the surface is clean.

STEP 2. With prepared pulp, do the basic hand papermaking Steps 1 through 9.

STEP 3. Allow water to drain naturally from the sheet for two minutes. This will provide some stabilization of the sheet.

STEP 4. Pick up the new sheet and screen and turn them over. Gently put the new sheet down onto the board's surface.

STEP 5. Do the basic hand papermaking Steps 14 through 17.

STEP 6. Carefully peel off the couch sheet, leaving the new paper sheet adhered to the board's surface.

STEP 7. Leave the new paper sheet on the board's surface until it is dry.

STEP 8. When the sheet is dry, lift it carefully from the board's surface. If the new sheet will not release (it sticks), try to work it off by inserting a razor or knife blade between the sheet and the board's surface at various places around the sheet. Then continue to lift gently. The worst scenario is that release will not occur and the sheet will have to be removed piecemeal to clear the board's surface. Lessen release problems by prespraying the board's surface with silicone, but read the label about good ventilation during use, etc. Other release aids are cooking sprays such as Pam, and petroleum jelly. Wipe off all excess aid before applying the sheet.

NOTE: Repeating the basic hand papermaking Steps 16 and 17 for removal of water can hasten drying.

 ARNOLD GRUMMER'S COMPLETE GUIDE TO EASY PAPERMAKING

Air Drying

Air drying produces a soft sheet with a variegated surface. Brushes and perhaps some fiber point pens can be used to write or draw on it. From an art standpoint, the surface produced by unfettered shrinkage forces can be highly dramatic. The precise nature of the air dried surface can vary widely, depending on the pulps used for the sheet, the rate of drying (high or low relative humidity, etc.), and whether or not any type of restraint is placed on the surface during drying.

Left totally unrestrained, shrinkage forces characteristic of the sheet's pulp will determine the final form, which can range from relatively flat to extremely curled. Almost always, the surface will not be very smooth. Sometimes sheet flatness can be maintained by putting weights on either end of the papermaking screen during drying. Should the sheet's nature be such that it will not let loose of the screen during drying, the weights will prevent the screen from being pulled into a curl and the final dried sheet will be flat. A window screen or very light cloth can be placed over the sheet in relaxed tautness and weighted on either end.

As with most techniques, air drying is a great field for experimentation.

STEP 1. Do the basic hand papermaking Steps 1 through 9.

STEP 2. Set the papermaking screen, with the wet sheet on it, somewhere to dry.

STEP 3. Let it dry solely by evaporation.

ALTERNATIVE: The above totally unrestrained air drying can be modified if desired. In Step 2, the screen and sheet can be pulled across the surface of a wrung-out sponge, removing some water. Little or much water can be sponged out before the sheet is set out to dry. Or the sheet can be set on or near a drying force such as a heat register, a sunny window, etc.

Examples of air dried sheets.

ARNOLD GRUMMER'S COMPLETE GUIDE TO EASY PAPERMAKING 102 ARNOLD GRUMMER'S COMPLETE GUIDE TO EASY PAPERMAKING

Air/Press Drying

Air/press drying creates a cameo, textured image area on an otherwise smooth surface, creating dimension. One procedure is described on the next page. Variations will likely occur to you after trying this project.

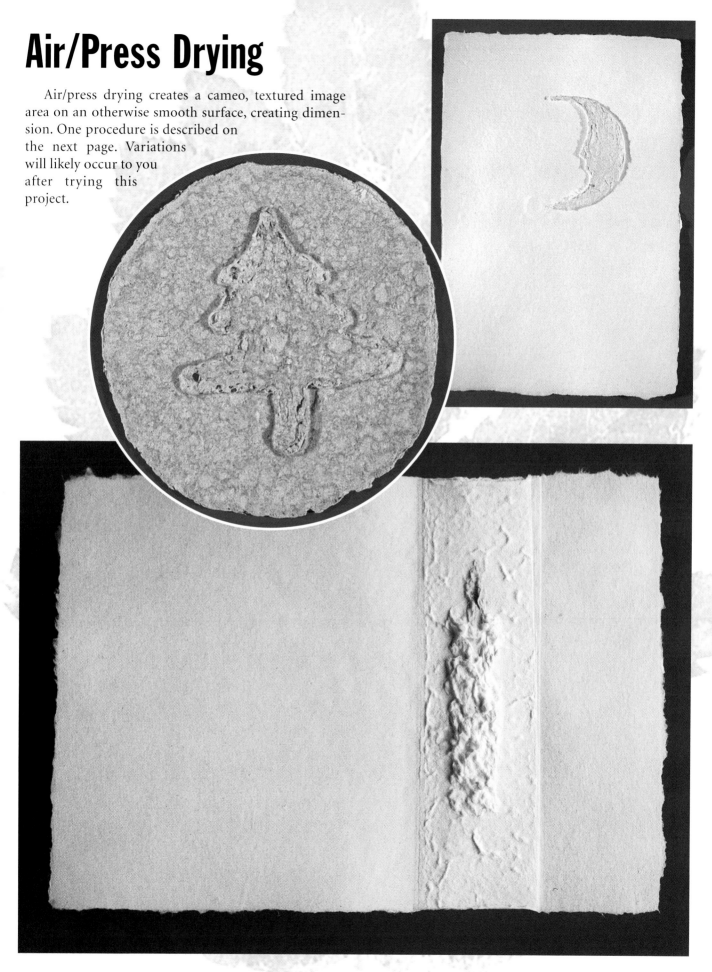

With an arrangement like this, the middle part of a green sheet will air dry while the other parts will be press dried.

STEP 1. Cut an image (tree, animal, heart, etc.) in a foam food tray or piece of wood. The foam board or wood must be at least as large as (preferably a bit larger than) the sheet of paper you're making.

STEP 2. Form a sheet of paper by doing the basic hand papermaking Steps 1 through 8.

STEP 3. Remove the papermaking screen and new sheet from the hand mold and place them on a drain rack or smooth surface.

NOTE: For experimentation, try adding a bit more pulp, possibly of another color, in the image area after Step 3.

STEP 4. Carefully place the foam board or piece of wood with the cutout image on top of the new sheet. Press down slowly and firmly. This will press down the covered part of the sheet but leave the image area at the original height.

STEP 5. Turn the assembled pieces (foam or wood, new sheet, screen) upside-down so the foam or wood is on the bottom and the screen on the top.

STEP 6. Remove water by pressing on the screen with a sponge.

STEP 7. Carefully remove the papermaking screen.

STEP 8. Place a couch sheet or couch material on the sheet.

STEP 9. Press down on the couch sheet until it has removed all the water it can.

STEP 10. Carefully remove the wet couch sheet and replace it with a dry one. When removing a wet couch sheet, the paper sheet might tend to rise with it. Use your fingernail or a knife to keep that from happening.

STEP 11. Again, turn the whole package over so the couch sheet is on the bottom and the foam or wood on top. Place a lightweight (book, container of water, brick, etc.) on the foam or wood board to provide pressure.

STEP 12. Change the couch sheet as it gets damp until the paper sheet is dry.

NOTE: The dry sheet should have a surface where part was dried under pressure and is smooth and part was air dried and is rougher.

ALTERNATIVE: More simply, make a sheet, remove it from the deckle, put a cover screen over only half of it, sponge only the half covered by the cover screen, remove the cover screen, put couch sheets over only that half, and put pressure for drying only on the couch sheets, permitting the other half of the sheet to air dry. Change couch sheets as they get damp until the sheet is dry.

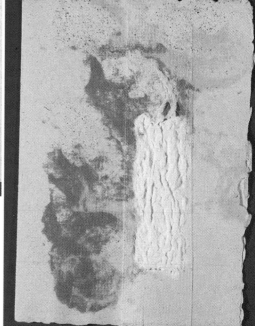

Glazing

This technique is very like Board Drying, but there are several differences. Glazed surfaces are fun to feel. They can reproduce more detail for stamping and are less prone to ink feathering.

STEP 1. Select a highly polished surface. The more polished the surface, the more the paper will be glazed. A photographer's ferrotype metal plate is excellent, as is any polished metal. A glass pane is good, but be extremely careful not to break it. Or try hard plastic countertops. Watch for shiny, polished surfaces.

STEP 2. Refer to Board Drying (page 100) and do Steps 2 through 9 except in Step 5, put the sheet down on a shiny surface.

NOTE: Read all the notes in Board Drying, especially the one regarding the problem of the sheet sticking to the surface.

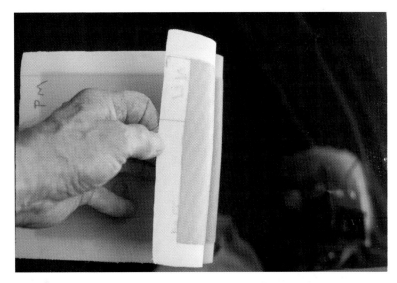

Ferrotype plate so shiny that the photographer can be seen.

The sheet being couched off onto the shiny cookie sheet.

The sheet on the cookie sheet surface.

Sheet Layering

This technique has almost everything in common with Pulp Layering (page 60) except here you are dealing with an entire sheet. This requires adept, more careful handling. But sheet layering offers its own effects. These include two-sided sheets, reinforcement of weak sheets, etc. This is a good technique to remember when it's necessary to patch a very weak sheet or a sheet with thin spots or holes in it.

It is another field that offers a great deal of exploration.

The two sides of a sheet after sheet layering.

This sheet was made by sheet layering a white sheet onto a colored sheet.

STEP 1. Prepare white pulp and do the basic hand papermaking Steps 1 through 10, but don't put the cover screen on the new sheet.

STEP 2. Prepare colored pulp. Using a second screen, do the basic hand papermaking Steps 1 through 9.

STEP 3. Lift the screen and colored sheet from the hand mold. While holding them, turn them over so the colored sheet is on the bottom side of the screen. The sheet is not likely to fall from the screen unless it is exceedingly wet and/or very thick. Generally, keep this colored sheet quite thin. It is also helpful to drag the screen and wet sheet over a wrung-out sponge (screen side on sponge) before turning the screen and sheet over.

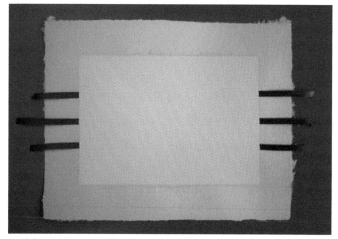

Ribbons layered between sheets.

STEP 4. Lower the colored sheet down on the white one, perfectly matching the edges of the two sheets. (You're right, perfectly matching the edges is difficult.)

STEP 5. Do the basic hand papermaking Steps 11 through 20. You should now have a sheet that is white on one side and colored on the other. Combine any two types of sheets you think would be exciting.

Self Bonding

Some exciting possibilities are offered by the fact that a batch of wet fibers will bond to another batch of wet fibers in the same way that a single fiber will bond to another fiber. Among other things, it permits self bonding an area of one handmade sheet to an area of another, making a rather impressive card. Reading through the instructions can jump start your imagination to other and greater things.

This is a variation on self bonding. These strips, when newly formed and wet, were laid down partially or completely overlapping each other. Pressed and dried, they self bonded into a single sheet.

STEP 1. Form a wet sheet by doing the basic hand papermaking Steps 1 through 10, but don't put on the cover screen.

STEP 2. Lay a piece of thin fabric as large as the sheet over the new sheet so that along one side, a 1/4″ to 3/8″ strip from top to bottom is not covered.

STEP 3. Using a piece of window screen, repeat Step 1, forming a second wet sheet.

STEP 4. Pulp layer (page 60) the second sheet onto the first. Because of the fabric laid over the first, the two wet sheets will touch only along the uncovered strip on one side. They will bond here.

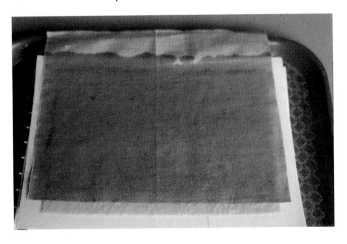

A cloth is put over a blue wet sheet except for a narrow strip at one edge where a second wet sheet will self bond to it. The self-bonding strips can be made as wide as you wish.

The two sheets are self bonded at the edge where the thumb is. Everywhere else they are free from each other, making a two-sheet, four-page leaflet, card, or letter with much room for stamping, drawing, words, etc.

A wet yellow sheet is sheet layered onto the partially covered blue sheet. The two sheets will touch, and therefore bond, only where the blue sheet has been left uncovered. The cloth can be left between the sheets through pressing and drying.

STEP 5. Treating the pulp layered sheets as a single sheet, do the basic hand papermaking Steps 11 through 20, leaving the fabric in place all the way through drying.

STEP 6. Open the dry sheets. Remove the fabric. You have an impressive card, leaflet, four-page series of art, or a longer letter, etc. The two sheets will have self bonded.

NOTE: As with any attempt to bond batches of pulp, greater pressure during pressing is effective. The more pressure applied, the better. And the longer it is applied (by using non-heat drying), the better.

Napkin Recycling

Napkins are a different kind of paper and recycling them can produce a different kind of effect. The result will likely be a sheet with a rich mosaic of small differently colored bits. The effect can be varied by running the blender for different lengths of time, by selecting different colors of napkins, and by varying the ratio of one color to another.

STEP 1. Select different colored napkins for recycling. The colors you select are an important factor in the kind of paper you'll achieve. The balance of bright to dark colors will determine the overall brightness or darkness of the paper made. It is an effect that is very noticeable.

STEP 2. Tear up the napkins and put them in the blender. Add water until the blender is full. Because of their nature, napkins need more water when being recycled.

STEP 3. Run the blender until only tiny chunks of napkin remain.

STEP 4. Make a sheet of paper by doing all of the basic hand papermaking steps.

For this effect, an illustration was cut from a napkin like that in the foreground. The rest of the napkin was recycled into a sheet. When the sheet was newly formed and wet, the illustration was placed on its surface. The sheet was then pressed and dried. This form of surface embedment is possible because of the nature of the napkin structure.

Examples of napkin recycling.

Watermarking

Sometimes, when paper is held up to light, an image can be seen in the paper. This image is a watermark. When the paper is thinner in an area, more light can pass through that area. If you can make your paper thinner in selected areas, you can make a watermark.

Watermarks have a fascinating history. They have been an item of mystique since 1282 A.D. They are still used for identification, authentication, anti-counterfeit and anti-fraud, and artistic expression. You haven't really lived until you have created your own watermark.

There's primitive technology in watermarks. Bend a wire into an image or form an image with something flat and not too broad. Secure it to the face of a papermaking screen and make a sheet. Where the image was on the screen, the paper will be thinner. Held to the light, the sheet will show a uniform brightness except where the paper is thinner. There, more light will come through, showing a replica of the image on the screen's surface. Behold a watermark!

There's also advanced technology in watermarks. They can be made to appear darker or shaded and dimensional like a photograph. They can be made with nothing visible on the screen. They can be created with modern photochemical processes. A look-alike mark can be put chemically in paper after the paper is dry.

A shaded Fabriano Madonna watermark from Italy. (Photo courtesy of the Robert C. Williams American Museum of Papermaking.)

There's romance in the watermark. It bears an aura of mystery and the supernatural: now you see it, now you don't. There is secrecy to a degree because many people are not aware of watermarks. One historical writer claims watermarks were a secret way of communication for a persecuted religious minority. In Europe, lesser paper mills counterfeited the watermarks of greater mills and sold lesser papers at greater prices. In crime, watermarks have undone criminals seeking to gain from fraudulent documents. An image of grapes has been immortalized as a watermark in paper of Gutenberg's Bible. Art of the Vatican lives in light-and-dark in the amazing shaded Fabriano watermarks of Italy. And Queen Elizabeth is presented majestically in her shaded Coronation watermark made by Portals of England.

A shaded Japanese watermark, "Sailboat by Moonlight." (Photo courtesy of the Robert C. Williams American Museum of Papermaking.)

Queen Elizabeth shaded watermark by Portals of England. (Photo courtesy of the Robert C. Williams American Museum of Papermaking.)

Watermark exhibit sheet showing a variety of types of watermarks. Damage at the lower left was initiated by water.

So, welcome to the club. Make your own watermark. Secretly communicate with another, even though you aren't persecuted.

Easiest, simplest, and most immediate is the first method presented below. The idea first occurred to me many years ago while at The Institute of Paper Chemistry. It should provide a lot of people with a lot of fun. Theoretically, a whole letter could be written in watermark! But there are some factors, such as sheet uniformity, that might work against it.

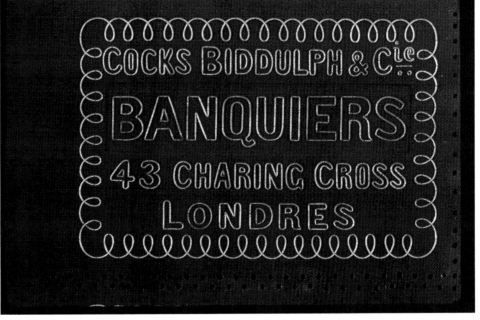

A professional hand-bent watermark on a hand mold used in a commercial hand-made paper mill.

Plastic Letters

STEP 1. Choose some 1/2″ plastic, self-adhesive letters from an office supply store. Select a word (or two or three) for a watermark. "SMILE" is easy for a first effort. (I like "DON'T PANIC.")

STEP 2. Apply the letters to the face of the papermaking screen. Leave 1/4″ between the letters. Will the letters stick? Usually. Roll over them with a rolling pin after they are on the screen. How long will they stay after being dunked in water? I've had varying luck, some staying a long time, others a short time.

STEP 3. Using the screen with the watermark, do all the basic hand papermaking steps and make a sheet.

NOTE: Paper thickness is of great importance when using plastic letters for a watermark. If the paper's too thick, the mark doesn't show. If too thin, the mark makes a hole in the paper. Keep adjusting until the thickness is right.

Plastic letters on the screen.

The watermarked sheet.

Ultimately Easy Two Toothpicks

This is simply an exercise in the sense of watermarking, though it can deliver a delightful and clear mark. Primarily, it gives you the sense of how the first mark was sewn onto the face of a papermaking screen. Also, for those not wanting to take the time to go further, the materials are easy to get and easy to use.

Step 1. Assemble two flat toothpicks, a needle and thread, contact cement, and a piece of window screen as big as your papermaking screen. (The window screen is suggested because you might not want to use your papermaking screen for your first effort.) Contact cement can be messy. The contact cement is not necessary if you wish to secure your watermark to the screen solely by sewing. If so, disregard all subsequent directions about contact cement.

STEP 2. Glue and/or sew the two toothpicks onto the surface of the window screen in the form of a V.

Sparingly apply contact cement to one side of the toothpicks. If cement fills any screen pores to either side of the toothpicks, the water flow through the screen will be affected, to the detriment of the ultimate watermark. Contact cement must be handled carefully and neatly. With the needle and thread, tack the toothpicks to the screen rather than sewing along their entire length. A tack at each end and one in the middle should suffice. Abut the toothpick ends closely at the bottom of the V.

STEP 3. Following the basic hand papermaking steps, make a sheet of paper using the window screen as the papermaking screen.

NOTE: Take particular care in Step 15 as the two toothpicks are raised out of the newly formed sheet with removal of the screen to which they are attached. If the watermark in the final sheet is too obvious, make a little thicker sheet. If it is too dim or hard to see, make the sheet thinner.

STEP 4. Hold your sheet to the light and look through it.

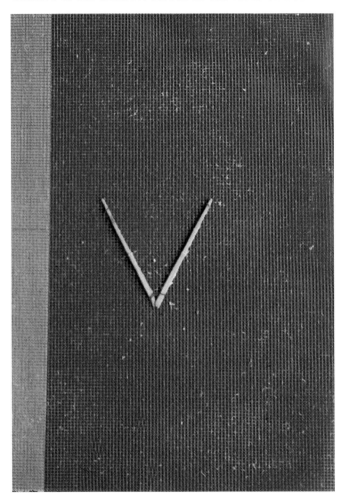 

At left, two toothpicks are sewn onto a papermaking screen. A sheet formed on it shows the watermark at right.

Plastic Twist, Solder, Etc.

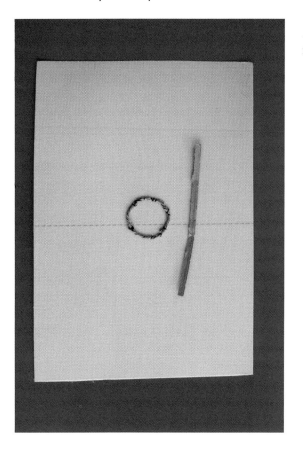

At left, the plastic twist lying on the screen was rolled into a round shape, bent into a circle, and sewn to the screen. At right is seen a watermark showing in a sheet made on the screen.

At left, a papermaking screen with a hand bent solder watermark and the tools that were used. At right, the watermarked sheet made on the screen.

In this project, the watermark image will be hand bent. This requires an easily bent material. Easily available is a plastic twist which can be left flat or made round by rolling up the plastic around the thin wire in the center. I recommend the latter. The best material I've found for bending watermarks is coiled solder, readily available at radio stores, hardware stores, etc. It is immensely malleable. Mistakes in bending are easily corrected and its range of diameters is reasonably compatible with desirable paper thickness.

While freehand bending is suggested, bending into specific images can be aided with nails pounded into a board. The nails are placed in the outline of the image. Try a simple triangle. Wire or other watermark material is then bent around the nail outline. Coiled solder is so malleable it can be bent around images such as cookie cutters, etc.

STEP 1. Start with two short plastic twists or one long one.

STEP 2. Twist the flat material into a round shape around the center wire.

STEP 3. Bend the rolled up twist into a circle. Twist the two ends together.

STEP 4. Glue or sew the circle to the surface of a papermaking screen.

NOTE: If sewing, tacking the circle down at about four places will likely suffice. You must tack it securely enough so no pulp flows beneath the watermark.

STEP 5. Following the basic hand papermaking steps, make a sheet of paper. Exercise care when lifting the watermark screen from the new sheet.

STEP 6. Hold your sheet to the light and look through it.

ALTERNATIVE: This project can be repeated with solder instead of plastic twists. Go to Step 3 and bend the solder into a circle, abutting the ends. Then simply follow the rest of the directions. Other possible watermark materials are small diameter electrical wires (with or without the insulation removed) and certain fairly rigid decorative cords. Keep an eye open for others.

You can use insulated radio wire or plant stems to form shapes.

To help make shapes, use nails in a board.

Screen on Screen

Not too difficult is a screen-on-screen watermarking project. It can have somewhat of the feel of a shaded watermark. It is done by cutting an image out of one screen and sewing it to the face of another.

Example 1

STEP 1. Cut an image out of a piece of papermaking screen. For a first effort, keep the image not more than 3″ high or wide.

A watermarked sheet made with a papermaking screen on a papermaking screen.

STEP 2. With needle and thread, sew the image to the face of your mold's papermaking screen.
STEP 3. Make a sheet of paper, following the basic hand papermaking steps.
STEP 4. If your watermark image is too dim, make another sheet with less pulp. If it is too light or has made a hole in your sheet, make a new sheet with more pulp. The image screen's thickness by itself will make a mark. If the image screen is also of different weave and/or material, that will help. If you have sufficient papermaking screen, you might want to use one screen just for cutting out images. If you don't have extra papermaking screen, sew three layers of window screen onto a papermaking screen, or, to a lesser degree, onto another window screen, and make a mark. It is not too difficult to cut an image out of three layers of window screen. Or reverse the materials and sew an image cut from papermaking screen onto the surface of a window screen.

Screen-on-screen watermarking is a fertile field for exploration. The following project will clarify the procedure for using window screen on a papermaking screen. It will not harm the papermaking screen should you later remove the watermark.

Example 2

STEP 1. Stack three pieces of window screen on top of each other.
STEP 2. Cut a simple three-layer image from them, perhaps a triangle.
STEP 3. Keeping their edges carefully lined up, tack the three layers together with needle and thread.
STEP 4. Sew the three-layer image to the face of a papermaking screen by tacking it down around its edges and at one place in the middle.
STEP 5. Make a sheet by doing the basic hand papermaking Steps 1 through 20. Make the sheet of average thickness.
NOTE: If the sheet's watermark area is too thin or becomes a hole, make a new sheet thicker. If the image is too dim, make a new sheet thinner.
STEP 6. Hold your sheet to the light and look through it. There are other variations of watermarks. The image can be made to appear dark rather than light by putting a channel in the screen's surface. This technique generally requires a metal screen.

A watermarked sheet made with triple window screen on a papermaking screen.

The image can also be made to appear in continuous gradations from light areas to dark areas, looking like a photograph. This is called a shaded watermark. It is done by creating an image (like a carving) which can be translated onto the surface of something sufficiently hard that a metal screen can be impinged upon it, translating the image into the screen. Literally, the screen is embossed with the image. The difficulty of the process and the growing scarcity of metal papermaking screen is sufficient reason to leave the shaded mark beyond this book's intent. Readers wanting to know about it in detail can find extensive coverage of it in Dard Hunter's book listed in the Bibliography.

PART 3

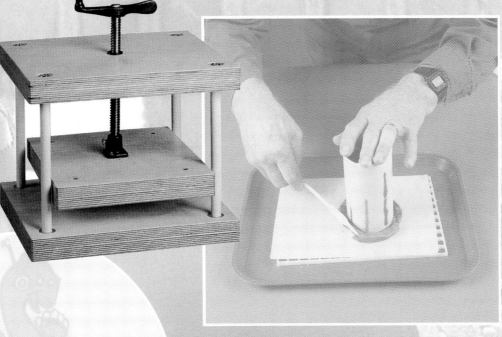

SPECIAL SHEETS

CHAPTER ELEVEN

Christmas Card with a Lighted Tree

Christmas is a very special time for handmade paper. Few things are more appropriate than a Christmas card that has its own lighted Christmas tree.

The Christmas tree here is a bit of arborvitae, but can be anything equivalent in appearance. The lights are bits of colored pulp applied with the point of a pin. It cannot be heat dried. This is one of my very favorite sheets.

STEP 1. Prepare white pulp for a handmade sheet of card thickness.
STEP 2. Select a bit of arborvitae that looks like a miniature Christmas tree.
STEP 3. Surface embed (see Surface Embedment, page 86) the piece of arborvitae on the right-hand side of the new sheet made with the white pulp.
NOTE: Surface Embedment offers two ways to do this.
STEP 4. Prepare a small amount of one or all of the following colored pulps: red, green, yellow, and blue.
STEP 5. Dip the point of a pin in a colored pulp, picking up just a very small bit of pulp on the tip.
STEP 6. Moving to the Christmas tree, apply the bit of colored pulp as a light on the arborvitae. Continue applying colored lights with all the colored pulps until you have a suitably lighted Christmas tree.
STEP 7. Do the basic hand papermaking Steps 10 through 17.
STEP 8. Place the sheet between dry couch sheets or other absorbent materials and put it under pressure in a press or under weight such as a stack of books. Change the couch sheets as they get damp until the sheet is dry.
STEP 9. Fold the dry sheet into a card with the Christmas tree on the front.

Applying a "light."

Sideliner Sheet

The Sideliner Sheet can be very beautiful for stationery, calligraphy, award certificates, settings for stamps or art. It is a sheet with a decorative or art strip down one side. It is an application of deckle division or pulp layering.

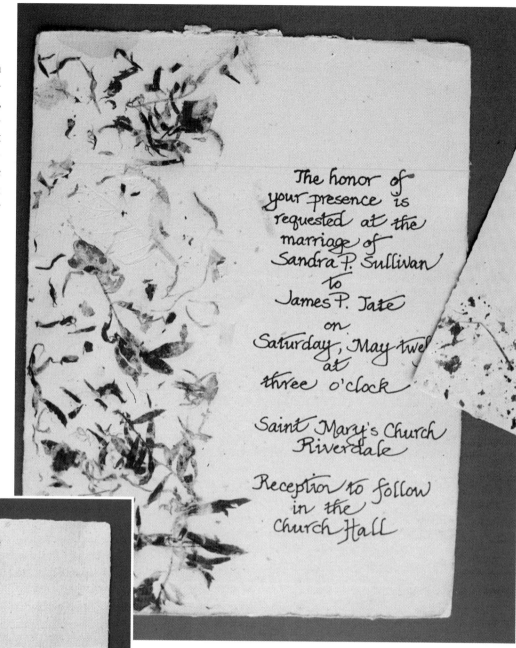

The honor of your presence is requested at the marriage of Sandra P. Sullivan to James P. Tate on Saturday, May twel... at three o'clock

Saint Mary's Church Riverdale

Reception to follow in the Church Hall

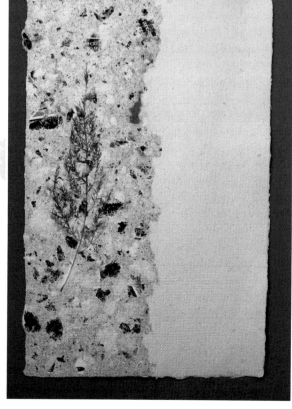

Project 1

STEP 1. Do Steps 1 through 5 of deckle division (page 92), but make the deckle divider for the long side of your hand mold's deckle instead the short side.

STEP 2. Slide the divider into your deckle about 1½″ from the deckle's left side. Place the deckle into the vat.

STEP 3. Prepare enough white pulp for the larger of the two compartments in the deckle. Pour it gently into the mold.

STEP 4. Prepare enough pulp for the smaller compartment. Pour it gently into the mold.

STEP 5. Add color or inclusions to the pulp in the small compartment.

NOTE: In Steps 4 and 5 creativity and imagination come into play. A different colored pulp can be used in Step 4. In Step 5, botanicals and other inclusions can be added in profusion or sparingly. Other colored pulps can be added. Glitter 'n glisten might be added. Some or all of these can make a striking, effective side strip on the new sheet.

STEP 6. Do Steps 10 through 13 of deckle division.

Project 2

STEP 1. Do the basic hand papermaking Steps 1 through 10, but don't put on the cover screen.

STEP 2. Do Steps 1 and 2 of Project 1, using a piece of window screen as the papermaking screen.

STEP 3. Prepare white or colored pulp and pour it into the small compartment of the deckle.

STEP 4. Add to the pulp whatever inclusions and/or colored pulps you desire.

STEP 5. Lift the mold from the water. After all water has drained, carefully lift the deckle divider. Be sure to lift the deckle divider straight out. Otherwise the edge of the pulp strip will be distorted.

STEP 6. Do the basic hand papermaking Steps 8 and 9.

STEP 7. Do Steps 7 through 10 of pulp layering (page 60), placing the pulp strip along one edge of the new sheet.

Moonscape

The success of this sheet depends on your ability to identify the right paper for recycling. The right paper is one that is heavily clay coated and bears huge expanses of deep colored ink. Heavy clay coating is identified by high gloss, i.e., a shiny paper.

Because paper can be given a glaze without clay, the gloss and shine must be outstanding—the glossiest and shiniest you can find.

With the right paper, much foam will occur in the blender during recycling. This indicates a clay formula coating. Foam remains when the pulp is poured into the deckle. When the deckle is raised and the foam on the pulp sinks toward the screen, the foam bubbles start bursting. Each burst sprays out minute clay particles colored by the ink. The bigger the bubble, the more obvious the effect.

Success is dependent on identifying the right paper to recycle and keeping the bubbles intact until they are down near the screen. When these two conditions are met, a quite spectacular visual surface is made.

Matched stationery. The envelope was made with a double deckle.

STEP 1. Do the basic hand papermaking Steps 1 through 4. After Step 4, the hand mold in the vat should be ready to receive pulp.

STEP 2. Find extremely shiny (slick) paper with an expanse of deep ink on it. Magazine covers and interior pages are good hunting grounds as are slick advertising pieces.

STEP 3. Recycle the paper in a blender with water. After a short time on a low speed, turn the blender up to high speed. There should be some foam generated.

STEP 4. As rapidly as possible, turn the blender off, pour the recycled pulp into the hand mold, and lift the hand mold out of the water. Do this rapidly so the least amount of foam bubbles dissipate before the pulp has drained down onto the screen.

NOTE: In the best case, many small bubbles and a number of large ones will burst as the pulp reaches the screen. Not every attempt achieves great success.

STEP 5. Do the basic hand papermaking Steps 8 through 20.

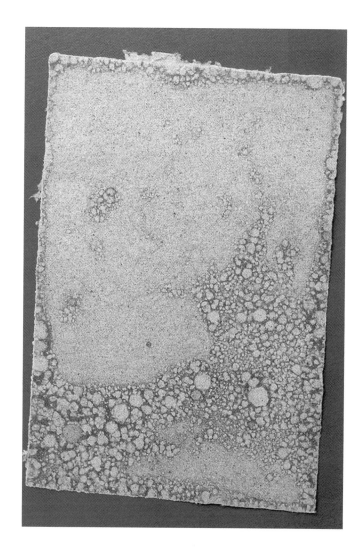

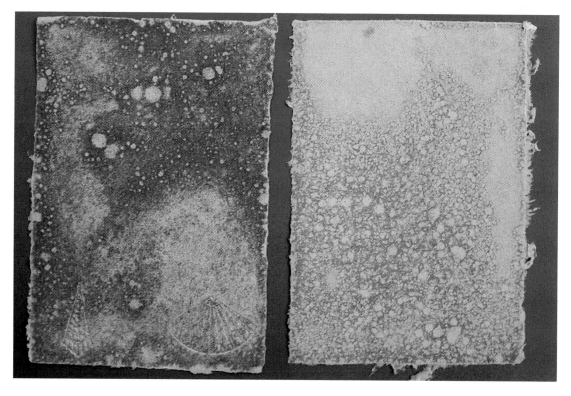

Word Surface

The mottle technique can be applied to several types of printed papers, photographs, etc. A quite striking handmade sheet can be made by applying it to a sheet densely printed on both sides. A pop culture sheet can be made by applying it to pages of the Sunday comics. Basically it is the mottling technique (page 52) carried to an extreme.

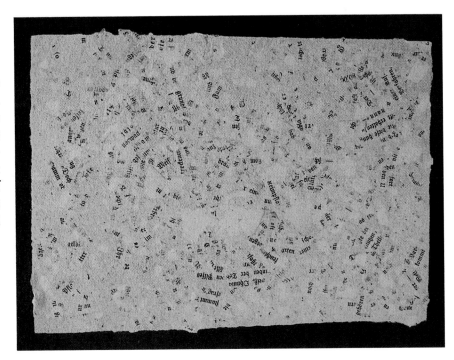

STEP 1. Find paper for recycling that is densely printed on both sides.

STEP 2. Blend 3″ squares of the paper in the blender until all chunks have disappeared.

STEP 3. Do the basic hand papermaking Steps 1 through 4.

STEP 4. Pour the pulp from the blender into the hand mold.

STEP 5. Put the rest of the densely printed page into the blender with more water than usual. Don't tear the paper into small pieces. You will want big pieces on the surface of your handmade sheet. If you tear the paper into small pieces for the blender, big pieces will not be available.

NOTE: For any mottling technique, recycle a bit more paper than usual for a new sheet.

STEP 6. Set the blender on high. Run it for only a short burst. The length of time you run the blender is critical. Experiment. The paper should be broken down sufficiently to be formable into a new sheet, but not so much that you don't get the surface of words that is desired. Also try running the blender a bit longer at slower speeds.

STEP 7. Pour the blender contents into the hand mold. Do the basic hand papermaking Steps 6 through 20.

NOTE: In basic hand papermaking Step 6, use your fingers to get as even a dispersion as possible. When the mold has been lifted, it might be possible to hold it with one hand and use the other to manipulate some of the paper pieces during draining. Manipulation might also be possible after Step 9. When the sheet is dry, it should have much of its surface showing words, phrases, or parts of words.

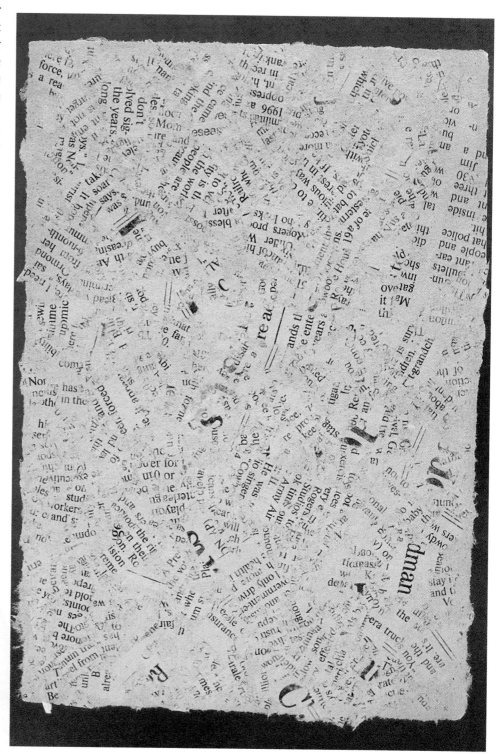

Sun Catcher

Sheet layering (page 106) can be employed to make a sun catcher. Put something appropriate between the pulp layered sheets that will be highlighted when the pulp layered sheets are put in front of light. It can be sort of a faux watermark. This technique could be applied to lampshades, etc.

This project should open the door to your imagination. What else can be laid between layered sheets? Try a gold ribbon longer than the sheets. Or decorative strings extending beyond the sheet's edges for tying a bow to close a greeting card. It's another great world for creativity, decoration, and art.

The finished sheet held up to light.

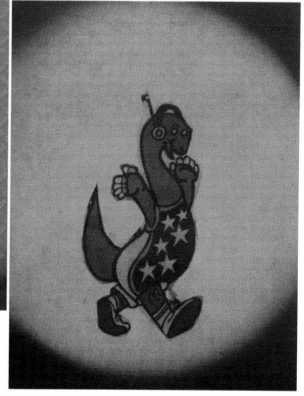

The design was cut from waste plastic packaging and laid on a wet sheet.

The completed sun catcher after the second sheet was sheet layered over the first, then pressed and non-heat dried.

STEP 1. Find colored images on transparent plastic (such as bread bags, etc.). Single items or sections from various packaging can be cut out and assembled in a montage. Or draw your own design on thin transparent plastic.

NOTE: Any single piece of plastic must not be too big. Several smaller pieces are better than one large one. You'll see why as you work through these directions.

STEP 2. Do Step 1 of sheet layering (page 106).

STEP 3. Place the plastic item(s) carefully on the new sheet's surface. It now becomes obvious that where the plastic pieces are laid, there will be no bonding between layered sheets. Too large an expanse can result in a bubble in the final sheet which is visually disturbing. Therefore, the smaller the pieces laid between the sheets, the better.

STEP 4. Using white pulp, complete the steps in sheet layering.

A SPECIAL PROJECT

CHAPTER TWELVE

Pencil Can

Sometimes art meets utility so that the art is not just hung isolated on a wall, but enters a personal intimate proximity as an item of some utility. Behold the lowly but lofty Pencil Can.

Making this item consists of wrapping a wet sheet of handmade paper around an appropriately selected and prepared can and letting it dry.

Cans that hold frozen fruit concentrate are often fiber rather than metal. A pencil holder can be made by stripping off the can's outer layer of printed fibers to expose the layers of cellulose fibers that make up the can's walls. When these walls are wet, they will bond to a degree to any wet handmade sheet wrapped around them (sheet layering). The whole mass will dry into a very fine can to hold pencils or anything else you choose. Whatever decoration you put on the layered sheet's surface before or after layering will be the can's exterior.

All techniques that can be applied in the blender, deckle, or after the sheet has been formed can be used. The opportunity for personal expression is unlimited.

STEP 1. Soak a fiber can in water for three to five minutes. Many frozen juice concentrate cans are fiber-bodied. Scratch a bit of the outer layer of printed fibers loose at the top edge and carefully peel the fiber layer off.

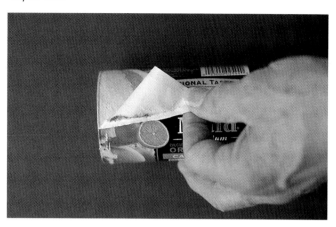

STEP 2. Choose any technique or combination of techniques and form a new handmade sheet, doing the basic hand papermaking Steps 1 through 11. In Step 11, remove only enough water to make it possible to lift and handle the sheet. Do not remove more water than is necessary.

STEP 3. Rewet the fiber can by dipping it into water and position it so it can be wrapped with a new sheet. NOTE: The can must be placed to ease wrapping with a wet fragile sheet.

Option 1. Place the can on its side on a flat surface. Carefully pick up the new sheet by both ends (art side up). Bring the sheet's middle over the can.

Line up the sheet's edge so it's against and perfectly parallel to the metal rim at the can's bottom. Carefully lower the sheet to the can's surface.

The ends of the sheet will extend to the surface on which the can rests.

Option 2. Put one hand inside the can. With the other hand, lift the new sheet. Bring the non-art side of the sheet against the can. Manipulate the sheet so that its edge is against and parallel with the metal ring on the can's bottom.

Option 3. Find a paper tube that will fit snugly inside the can. Lay the tube on a table. with one end extending beyond the table's edge. Slip the can over the extended end of the tube.

Pick up the wet sheet. Drape it, art-side-up, over the can, with its bottom edge against and parallel to the metal rim at the can's bottom.

STEP 4. For Option 1, slip your hand inside the can. Lift the can with the paper draped over it. (Option 2 already has it lifted. Option 3 need not lift.) Place a thin cloth over the new sheet.

STEP 5. With your palm, brush gently over the cloth in a smoothing manner, with just a bit of pressure. Rotate the can until one end of the sheet has been smoothed onto the can. Rotate in the opposite direction until the other end is on the can's surface.

NOTE: If your sheet is long enough, the two sheet ends will overlap. In a 5½" x 8" mold, the sheet ends will be just short of meeting. In this case, add a little pulp with a pulp gun to one end of the sheet before putting the cover screen on in basic hand papermaking Step 10, or lay a thin strip of pulp down on a piece of screen with the pulp gun and pulp layer the strip onto the can, overlapping each end of the sheet. The effect can be enhanced by using a different color pulp.

STEP 6. Let the can air dry.

Base for the Pencil Can

Though not necessary, a base can be both functional and aesthetic.

STEP 1. Pile a round mound of very wet pulp on a surface (screen or otherwise). The mound should be 1/2" to 3/4" high and quite uniform in thickness. The pulp can be one or more colors with or without glitter 'n glisten, etc., and 1/2" to 3/4" greater in diameter than the can.

STEP 2. After Step 7 in the project above, set the bottom of the wrapped can precisely in the center of the pulp mound.

STEP 3. With a hand across the top of the can, force it down into the wet pulp mound. This will cause pulp to be higher than the can's bottom rim all the way around the can.

STEP 4. The base can be left to dry as is or manipulated as follows: Take a spatula or wide knife and brush the base's wet pulp up and against the can's sides. The base can be shaped as desired.

STEP 5. Let the can dry.

CASTING

Casting can be defined as the reproduction of a shape by means of a malleable material placed into the shape and left to harden. Think of filling an ice cream cone with wet plaster and letting it dry. The plaster will dry in the shape of the cone.

Wet pulp behaves similarly. The same pulp that makes a sheet can be arranged into any other shape. Laid out on a dimensional surface, wet pulp will dry into the shape of that surface.

Because of the minute size of the papermaking fiber, wet pulp can be worked into a surface's most minute details and crevices and will reproduce that detail or crevice when dry. Consequently, wet pulp is an ideal medium for casting.

The natural bond between fibers should be remembered. When casting, you will often press the pulp into the detail of the shape. This pressure removes water and strengthens the natural bond between fibers. Hence, when pressure is subsequently applied at point A to move fibers into details there, a chain reaction of natural bonds might be simultaneously affecting fibers at point B. This could explain some otherwise unexplainable and frustrating voids (pits) on the surface of dried castings.

The casting procedure is quite simple as evidenced by the following projects. When you've mastered these, you may want to try something more challenging.

Fibers: For surface castings, white fibers enhance detail more than colored—cotton linters work best. You can try using just recycled paper (white grocery bags are good) or a blend of recycled paper with cotton linter. For shape castings, any new or recycled white or colored fibers can be used, along with appropriate inclusions.

Molds: Molds are what you put or pour wet pulp around, into, or onto. Shape molds can be seashells, cookie cutters, muffin tins, candy molds, small trays,

any plastic food containers, or just about anything that catches your eye. Surface molds are surfaces presenting some image that might be highly or more

Each of these can be used to make a paper "shape." All are "found" except the tree shape (center) is a cutout in a food foam board. At upper left, a milk carton can make a square or, when squeezed in at two corners, a diamond. Shapes made with the cat and candle cookie cutters are shown in another illustration.

These are surface molds. At right and top are ceramic molds found at craft stores. At bottom left are cookie molds. Castings are shown with some of the ceramic molds.

subtly dimensional such as metal plates, bricks, etc. A wide variety of commercial molds can be found in art and craft stores. Look for carvings. Walking through junk stores can yield a variety of interesting glass and metal surfaces on plates, wall hangings, etc. Even a brick wall with textured bricks and deep grouting is interesting. Finally, shape and surface molds have been found in a series of cookie cutters. The world is full of interesting shapes and surfaces waiting for casting.

Applying Pulp to Molds: Shape molds can be filled with wet pulp in almost any manner.

For surface molds, the way pulp is applied will affect the quality of the dried casting. Pulp should be very wet so the individual fibers can move into mold detail. One application method is to form a very thick sheet in a hand mold. Using a pulp layering action, drop the sheet over the mold. Use minimal pressure to jiggle (short back and forth movements) the pulp into the smallest surface details. Another method is to pour pulp from the blender into a kitchen strainer, then apply the pulp to the mold in batches. For both methods, press the pulp firmly into the mold. You can apply pressure first with only a thin layer of pulp on the mold, then again after more pulp has been added, or wait until the desired thickness of pulp has been applied. In smaller molds, apply the pressure uniformly across the pulp with a board or your fingers.

Pressure forces water out of the pulp. You can either remove no water, starting the drying phase immediately, or you can sponge off water to reduce the drying time. Sponging exerts a slight pull on the fiber mass. Under some conditions, fibers at the mold's surface could be affected. The preceding are all options. Try them all. Use the one that works best for you.

Additives: A variety of additives can be used in casting pulp. These are said to yield firmer casting surfaces more suitable for painting and to provide other characteristics. Many of the additives come from the commercial paper industry. In some cases,

the name given the additive—such as stabilizer—is so general and ambiguous you really won't know what the additive does. In my opinion, additives are an unnecessary expense. Those from the paper industry are used under very controlled conditions. Their results are measured by highly scientific instruments.

Many additives have a shelf life. Used after that, they are not guaranteed effective by the manufacturer. Most additives packaged in small amounts (the paper industry buys huge quantities) are extremely expensive. However, anything put into pulp will have some kind of effect, subtle or gross. If you wish to explore additives, purchase some and try them. If they produce a discernible effect on your casting, good. If not, don't waste your money. Be sure you get instructions and any expiration information from your vendor. Obviously, it's important to know how long such an additive has been on the shelf.

Releasing the casting from the mold: In every individual casting, releasing the pulp from the mold is critical. Release occurs when the dry casting lets go of the surface of the mold as in Board Dryings and Glazing. Surface chemistry sometimes creates a powerful adhesion that is difficult to overcome. The result is a ruined casting. The problem can often be prevented by coating the surface with a release agent. Many people use non-stick cooking sprays such as Pam. I've had success with silicone spray (be sure to read the label). Petroleum jelly is another option. Some suppliers offer commercial release agents. Whatever you apply to the mold, wipe off all the excess before adding pulp.

Note: *Arnold Grummer's Complete Guide to Paper Casting* by Arnold and Mabel Grummer is available from Krause Publications.

Shape Project
Putting Pulp In a Form

Two cat shapes from another illustration pose here with other "shape" friends. The candle and bell were made with cookie cutters; the deer with an open cookie cutter; the sheep with a cookie mold; the round base and quarter moon with a tin can and a foam board cutout, respectively.

These cat shapes show that (a) a shape can be made with different colored pulps, and (b) shapes can be made to different thicknesses.

STEP 1. Select a shape (inverted seashell, open cookie cutter, any design cut out of some reasonably thick material). This becomes the mold.

STEP 2. Prepare sufficient pulp to fill the mold.

NOTE: A multicolor casting can be made if you prepare several pulp colors.

STEP 3. If the shape has no solid bottom (open cookie cutter), place it on a screen on a drain rack so that water can drain.

STEP 4. Pour pulp directly into the open shape. If the shape has a solid bottom (such as a seashell or cookie mold), first strain the pulp through a strainer, then put batches of pulp into the mold.

NOTE: If pouring pulp, pour the shape full, let it drain, then pour it full again. This is the only way to get reasonable thickness in the dried casting.

STEP 5. Removing water is not a must, but it will reduce the drying time. Step 6 can be done immediately, permitting nature to remove all water. This extends drying time. However, a different type of casting will result if water is removed by sponging or squeezing.

After taken from a strainer at left and applied to a surface mold, the pulp is partially de-watered with a sponge. Window screen can be kept between the sponge and pulp.

STEP 6. Place the casting where it will dry best (radiator, sun, outside in sun and wind). You can use a microwave oven to reduce drying time, but be very sure everything involved can be microwaved. Oven time depends on the casting thickness. Conventional ovens should be used, if at all, at very low heat, best with only the pilot light. Heat affects fibers.

STEP 7. When it is dried, remove the pulp casting from the mold. Normally this type of casting will offer minimal release problems.

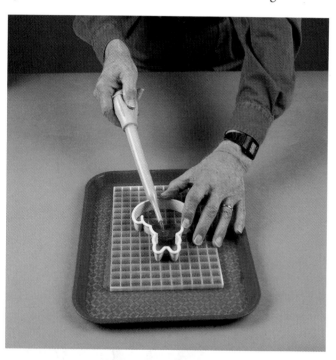

To be filled with pulp of one or more colors, this cat shape has been placed on window screen over a grid in a drain pan. The slurry in the baster should be kept sufficiently thin and the baster held at an angle. This can become a paper shape or be pulp layered onto a sheet.

Shape Project
Putting Pulp Around a Form

STEP 1. Select a shape to use as the mold. (Try any variety of small containers—round, square, oblong, deep or shallow. Food containers—fast food, plastic throw-away ice cream dishes, plastic cookie trays—can become excellent and useful castings.) Any and all shapes are fair game.

STEP 2. Apply release agent to the mold's surface.

STEP 3. Prepare sufficient pulp to cover the mold.

NOTE: A multicolor casting can be made if you prepare several pulp colors.

STEP 4. **Option 1.** Make thick sheets with a hand mold. By pulp layering, drape them over the shape. Continue making sheets until the shape is covered. With a spatula or similar tool, smooth the seams where the sheet edges overlap, using a soft stroking action. Additional sheets can be layered to achieve thickness of casting.

Option 2. Pour pulp into a kitchen strainer. Completely cover the mold in batches. Keep an eye on uniformity of covering thickness.

STEP 5. Do Steps 5 through 7 of the project on page 136.

Plastic forms such as cookie package trays and ice cream parlor throw-away serving dishes make artful castings that are both interesting and useful.

The casting in the foreground was made from a contemporary plastic form such as shown in back.

Surface Project
Putting Pulp on a Surface

STEP 1. Select a surface for casting. (The surface should be dimensional to some degree).

STEP 2. Apply a release agent to the surface.

STEP 3. Prepare enough pulp to cover the surface.

NOTE: A multicolor casting can be made if you prepare several pulp colors.

STEP 4. Put pulp on the surface. See the options listed in Step 4 in the project above.

STEP 5. Work pulp into all details of the surface by jiggling and pressing as discussed above.

STEP 6. Do Steps 5 through 7 on page 136.

NOTE: Removing pulp casting from a surface often requires care, caution, and patience.

Found in a second-hand store, the embossed metal plate in back is an interesting casting subject. A craft store supplied the mold-making material for the casting mold at left, from which the pulp casting at right was made. Often the pulp can be applied directly to the casting subject. (Casting by Mabel Grummer.)

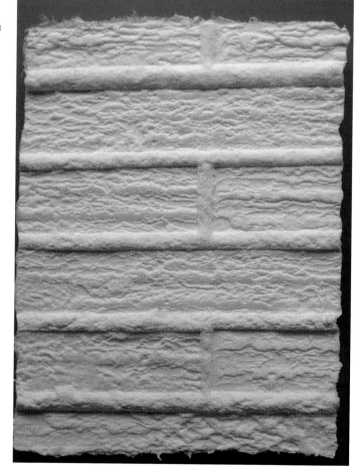

This was cast on a brick wall of my home.

VARIATIONS
FOR THE ADVENTUROUS
PAPERMAKER

CHAPTER FOURTEEN

Dyeing Paper

My initial reaction to dyeing paper is, "If you want to make decorative and artistic papers, what are you doing spending your time on dyeing?" All the colors, hues, and pastels of dyed fibers you can ever imagine are in your waste basket, free. Take them, and get to making beautiful papers. And remember—waste paper does not mean waste fiber. These fibers have been dyed professionally with high technology and expert supervision at pulp or paper mills. You are not likely to match their quality at home for some time, if ever.

Also, color for handmade paper is available by recycling papers printed with colored ink. Notice the subdued or brilliant inks on papers. Then put that color in your handmade papers by recycling the papers so colorfully printed.

If you want to try your hand at dyeing or if you absolutely must have what some natural dye offers, here are a few guidelines.

Realize first that the in-depth world of dyeing is hectic, made up of pots, pans, multi-hour soaks, hot and cold water, acidity and alkalinity, bleeding, light fastness, staining, direct dyes, fiber-reactive dyes, natural dyes, artist acrylic colors, plant and berry squishing and squashing, straining, lots of time, some expense, and more.

Try simpler, easier things first. Start with a fabric dye (such as Rit) and follow the directions. Or try food coloring. Add the coloring agent to the pulp and let it soak at least overnight. Alternatively, experiment with artist acrylic colors available at art supply stores. Put a bit in the blender with the fiber. Run the blender. Let the pulp soak with the color overnight.

Then try going natural. Find plants, berries, etc., that when squashed/squeezed and soaked and/or boiled in water, will color the water. Then soak pulp in the water. Try onion skin, marigold blossoms, elderberries, blueberries, grapes, dandelions, lilies of the valley, grass, mistletoe, or anything else that strikes your fancy. (Be prepared for some strong odors when boiling natural substances.)

I've also known people to try using powdered tumeric (spice), strong brewed coffee, and colored napkins (from which dye bleeds).

Most paper dyers use mordants to help fix the color. Use small amounts with each pulp batch. Mordants include salt, vinegar, soda, alum, and tannic acid.

But don't forget. If the color will get into your pulp, it might get into your equipment too. Use pots, pans, vats, etc. that are expendable or that you will still be able to use if they absorb the color. Wear something over good clothes. Dedicate a number of your couch sheets for use just with dyed papers.

If all of this interests you, check other papermaking books for specific recipes. My previous book, *Paper by Kids*, has some easy recipes and projects. Check especially *Papermaking* by Jules Heller or *Color for the Hand Papermaker* by Elaine Koretsky (see Appendix).

Other sources of information are arboretums, botanical gardens, and paper mills. Watch for any area papermaking dye workshops. Or, if you want to speed things up, just reach for your favorite color in your favorite waste basket. Remember, waste paper is not waste fiber.

Glitter 'n Glisten

Many people thrill to glitter and glisten in or on paper. Soft or brilliant reflections from a paper surface as it is turned at different angles to light can surprise, please, and delight.

A glitter 'n glisten sheet can be made by recycling envelopes with gold foil liners, packaging materials including foil in their makeup (some margarine boxes), wrapping that is totally foil (margarine stick wrappers), Christmas wrap that is partially foil or laminated to foil, etc.

A problem can arise in that foils often are pounded into small dense "wads" by the blender. Sometimes this doesn't matter, especially if drying is done without heat and under considerable pressure. It's also helpful to reduce the time the foil part of the paper is in the blender. Total flatness of foil pieces can be achieved by cutting the foil to desired sizes with scissors and introducing them into the pulp in the deckle (adding the foil after the pulp has been blended).

Other foil sources include gum wrappers, components of cigarette packages, cut-up aluminum foil, candy wrappers, and can and jar labels. Simply stated, foil is where you find it, attached or separate from paper. If you see it, try it.

Glitter also comes in near-powder form in bottles at your local craft store. Try them. Greg Markim, Inc. has searched internationally and found some glitters compatible with drying paper with heat (iron). This small-size flake or near-powder glitter can be added in either the blender or the deckle. The blender has an effect on some types, and none on others.

Some glitter 'n glisten can be achieved by recycling Christmas cards and other paper printed with metallic inks. The result success depends on the amount of ink in relation to the size of the paper or card and how heavy the metallic ink is.

In general, keep your eye out for glitter 'n glisten. When you see it, try recycling it or otherwise adding it to your handmade paper.

Paper from Plants or Pants?

Can you make paper out of your very own plants or pants? Yes, but do you really want to go to all the work and trouble? With plants, will you really have paper? And do you want to take the trouble and precautions involved with caustics?

Turning either your family grass and zinnias or your faded blue jeans into paper involves fuss and work, probably caustics, and patience.

Plants

Plants have the little cellulose fibers for papermaking. The problem lies in getting rid of the non-cellulosic part of the plant.

The general procedure is to reduce the plant to small pieces, soak the pieces (simmering and caustics like lye or soda ash help), rinse until the water runs clear (to rid the material of any dissolved non-cellulosic matter and caustics), beat the material with a mallet or other suitable device until it *feels* like pulp, and then make paper with the resulting pulp.

This is a very generalized procedure. For specifics, either experiment on your own or do some reading. John Mason's book is delightful and detailed and Vance Studley offers specifics in his book (see Bibliography).

After conquering the plant, do you have paper? You will have a mat, certainly. It will be decorative and very likely aesthetically interesting. Its usability beyond framing or other passive existence might be very limited. However, it will be your own grass and zinnias.

Pants

Turning fabric into paper is really not an at-home project. The fabric must be undone all the way back to the original fibers which were woven into threads, which in turn were woven into fabric. The undoing requires an immense amount of powered beating. Industry has developed a mechanical beater which endlessly submits the fabric (in water) to a grinding passage between two metal surfaces, one of which is metal bars on a turning cylinder. Even with high-tech design and immense electrical horsepower, turning fabric into pulp is not a short run. Matching both high-tech design and horsepower with hand power at home is more than daunting. Not that it's impossible—the first Chinese papermakers did it.

Were you to insist on giving it a whirl, you would have to think like those Chinese (and exercise their patience and stamina). You would first need some kind of mortar and pestle arrangement. Then cut the fabric into small pieces and put the pieces into the mortar with water. With a continuous raising and lowering of the pestle, stamp until the fabric is reduced to individual fibers. Finally, make paper with the resulting fibers.

Presoaking with some caustic helps, but necessitates washing and rinsing operations and equipment. Retting (keeping the fiber damp for a long period of time) helps, but can induce discoloration.

I recommend simply taking your fabric to a papermaker, papermaking studio or center, and having it run in a beater. Then take the pulp home and make paper from your very own blue jeans.

Selective Recycling

Selective recycling can produce a number of art and decorative sheets. For myself, handmade papers produced fall generally into three types: Type 1—art or decorative; Type 2—"I've always wanted a sheet recycled from _____"; and Type 3—soul. Some examples are listed below. You will discover others yourself.

Art or Decorative

* Slick, shiny (clay coated) papers with expanses of one color of ink make "Moonscape" sheets (page 122).
* Food can or jar labels for beautiful mottled surfaces (page 52): Bush's Baked Beans printed in heavy copper/bronze ink; V-8 Juice; Morton's Iodized Salt blue wrapper; colorful microwave popcorn sacks—your eyes will pick out more.
* Colorful wrap with metallic ink or foil. Colorful (corrugated) light bulb cartons.
* Ream wrappers for printing and copy papers (these sometimes contain a thin film moisture barrier which can become a very subtle highlight on a handmade sheet's surface).

"I've always wanted a sheet recycled from _____"

* Yellow Pages
* Pages from a favorite book
* Canceled domestic, foreign, or Christmas stamps
* Photographs
* My 1941 high school graduation awards
* Newspapers announcing historic events such as sinking of Titanic, moon landing, Charles and Diana's wedding, newspaper editorial, etc.

Soul

Early Chinese papermakers believed that if a sheet bearing a love poem from a loved one was recycled into a new sheet, the words and love expressed on the original sheet remained resident in and among the fibers of the new sheet. A poem of love was then written on the new sheet and returned to the sender.

When recycled, certain pieces of paper lend "soul" (a special feeling) to the new handmade sheet. A paper's use, what was on it or who it was from, can transfer a special, spiritual quality and feeling to a sheet recycled from it.

To recognize this, it helps to be a bit of a romantic, sentimental, over sensitive, easily touched, and given to easy crying. For those who are, a handmade sheet made from recycled Christmas cards and letters from a favorite aunt, or canceled Christmas stamps, or newspaper photos of a favorite movie star or football quarterback, will have its own special persona.

This is an example of paper that has "soul." It is a pastor's bookmark for his Bible. The white cross symbolizes the timelessness of his message because it is made of 100% 11,000-year-old tree fiber. There is joy in the red circle because it is recycled Christmas card envelope and the color represents the redeeming blood of Jesus Christ. The blue is 100% cotton denim, the working clothes of the masses, for whom the pastor's message is meant.

PART
4

HINTS AND HELPS

CHAPTER FIFTEEN

Fast and Slow Draining Pulps

Some pulps, recycled or new, drain more slowly than others. This is often because of fiber length and amount of beating. Slow draining pulps are invaluable for some techniques, especially surface embedment. When a pulp drains slowly, identify what was recycled. Then when you want a slow draining pulp, you will know what to recycle. Release papers, which are what self-adhesive labels are peeled from, general-ly recycle into a slow draining pulp. Newsprint does too, but the ink can discolor papermaking screens, etc.

Pure (Unprinted) Paper for Recycling

Most of the time, sheets of beautiful white or colored paper are covered with printing. But beautiful, unencumbered fibers can be salvaged by cutting away unprinted margins and other areas. If you hold the sheet up to light, you can see where the printing is on both sides and easily cut away the unprinted paper for pure white or color clippings for recycling.

Writing on Mottled Surfaces

The mottled surface technique can make impressive handmade papers and greeting cards. But they can be difficult or impossible to write on. The writing gets lost in the mottling. With a turkey baster, lay a thin even layer of solid white or colored pulp on a second screen, then pulp layer it onto the mottled surface. This provides a writing patch. It can be made in different shapes.

Moving Wet Sheets from One Surface to Another

When a mat of wet fibers is placed between two surfaces and pressure is applied, it will generally stay with the smoother of the two surfaces when the surfaces are parted.

Botanical Difficulties

Botanicals frequently float to the top and thus evade becoming tied down to the sheet surface. While pulp is draining, carefully push the botanical beneath the surface of undrained pulp. Be careful

ARNOLD GRUMMER'S COMPLETE GUIDE TO EASY PAPERMAKING   147   ARNOLD GRUMMER'S COMPLETE GUIDE TO EASY PAPERMAKING

not to push so hard that fibers already on the screen are too much disturbed, which could seriously or fatally flaw the sheet.

Some botanicals leach out plant elements during drying, creating a corona of stain-like color in the dried sheet. This can be attractive or unattractive. It sometimes seems that the less time the botanical is wet, the less the corona. For such foliage, drying with an iron would be best. With some foliage, soaking ahead of time seems to help. Some foliages seem to leach hardly at all. Consequently, it's hard to generalize. Making test sheets can be helpful. Dry one sheet slowly under pressure and a second sheet with an iron. Soak some of the same foliage in advance to see whether presoaking helps. Again, personal experience and observation are your best teachers. May Nature be kind to all of us.

Long and Short Fibers

Short fibers drain more slowly and provide less strength in a handmade sheet. Long fibers (unbeaten) drain rapidly. They generally provide more strength in a sheet. Grocery and other sacks generally are made with long fibers. Groundwood papers (newsprint) generally provide very short fibers.

Hard and Soft Papers

Pressure during pressing is a notable factor in making hard or soft handmade papers. For a very soft paper, form a sheet on a screen and let it air dry with no pressure. For a very hard sheet (crackly with a solid feel), mount as much pressure as you can during pressing. Pressure also congeals the surface, providing a somewhat better writing surface, some resistance to ink feathering, etc.

Turbulence for Sheet Uniformity

Turbulence in the deckle of a pour hand mold is important to the uniformity of the final sheet. Wiggling your fingers or creating turbulence some other way disperses the pulp evenly. Keeping a pour mold low in the vat's water also helps. For dip molds, agitate pulp before each dip.

Drying and the Teflon Iron

This book advocates placing a thin cloth between the wet paper sheet and the iron. However, many sheets are dried by placing the hot iron directly onto the wet sheet. This is a dangerous way to dry paper because a fiber(s) might adhere to the iron, and in two more strokes, the sheet surface can be seriously or fatally disrupted. If you don't use a cloth, add to the sheet's safety by using a Teflon-coated iron. Of course, even Teflon can't protect against materials melting in the sheet (bits of plastic ribbon, film, etc.).

Organize Waste Paper for Recycling

For efficiency, organize waste paper according to the kind of sheet to be made. These classifications might help: (1) white unprinted sheets or clippings (margins from letters, brochures, etc.) and envelopes purged of printing and clear windows; (2) colored unprinted sheets, pages, and clippings; (3) papers printed with bold colors of ink (including Christmas wrap) for great mottled papers; (4) specialties such as waxed bakery sacks, microwave popcorn sacks, ream wrappers, greeting cards with metallic ink; (5) newsprint; and (6) miscellaneous "interesting" and "want to try" papers.

QUESTIONS AND ANSWERS

CHAPTER SIXTEEN

Question: How do I dispose of the waste water after a session of papermaking? Can I pour it down the sink or toilet?

Answer: The sink, NO! The toilet, yes. The waste water will have sediment. Four minutes after the last disturbance of the water, you will see it at the bottom of the vat. The sediment will include broken and loosened bits of cellulose fiber and likely some non-fiber paper additive residue. This has great potential for becoming a clog in sink drains, but a toilet system can handle it. Stir the water well before dumping it.

Question: Can I make paper out of dryer lint?

Answer: Yes, if all or at least quite a few of the fibers/threads are natural (from plants). No natural fibers—no bonding. The problem is to get the lint dispersed in water. It tends to stay in clumps which can lead to lumps in paper. However, if there are many different colored threads, something quite nice can result. Try using smaller bits of lint as an accent in a regular sheet. All in all, lint is an experience and can make paper that is different, so go for it.

Question: What can be recycled?

Answer: Any paper. If it can't be recycled with water and a blender, it isn't paper. Of course, it doesn't make sense to try to recycle tar paper or paper laminated to some material.

Question: Can flowers and things (botanicals) be put in paper?

Answer: Yes, so long as their size (bulk) and shape are reasonably compatible with paper's structure. Some of the techniques in this book involve botanicals. (See "Botanical Difficulties" in the previous chapter.)

Question: What is the greenish-yellow stain that spreads around some of the leaves and flower petals put in paper?

Answer: I wish I knew exactly. I refer to it as a corona. I suspect it is plant elements like chlorophyll that water leaches out into surrounding (hydrophyllic) fibers. If that is true, the quicker the drying, the less corona. But to get the final answer, both of us should pursue the matter with qualified botanists and/or books. If you find the answer before I do, please write. (See "Botanical Difficulties" in the previous chapter.)

Question: Can I make paper out of my zinnias?

Answer: Not easily or rapidly, and only if you get them before the rabbits do (I know this from personal experience). See Paper from Plants and Pants, page 143.

Question: Does recycling hurt a blender?

Answer: Not any more than the normal wear that would occur from using it for any food purpose. If you put too much paper with too little water into the blender, it might burn out. But a similarly thick mix of food would too. A ratio of two cups of water to an amount of fiber represented by 3/4 of an 8½″ x 11″ sheet of typing paper will not likely harm a blender. Equally cogent is the question, "Can I use my blender for both paper recycling and food?" If cleaning is thorough and proper, and if general use ordinary paper is recycled, nothing that I know of would prohibit use for both. But, to protect myself against any possible liability, I hereby clearly recommend you not use one blender for both. Do as my Quarter Moon Mill does—go to garage and rummage sales and get good solid, heavy blenders for a couple dollars.

Question: What is the liquid in the vat (when paper is being made)?

Answer: Water. Just plain water. Anything else wouldn't work. The natural bond that makes paper possible is triggered only by water.

Question: What is a couch sheet?

Answer: A piece of material that will take a newly formed wet sheet off a papermaking screen in a manner that will not ruin the new sheet. If the couch sheet is also absorbent, it will help remove water as well as remove the sheet.

Question: Can I make paper out of my blue jeans?

Answer: See Paper from Plants and Pants, page 143.

Question: How can I get more of a feathered (deckle) edge?

Answer: Feathering of a deckle edge is done by water and fibers running out of the hand mold between the bottom of the deckle and the papermaking screen. A few fibers are caught between the deckle and the screen, but not many because there simply is not much room. When the few fibers involved form a continuous line of bonded fibers, they form a very thin, irregular extension to the main sheet.

It is a feathering effect which some people love and others can't stand. The effect is possible most easily with a pour mold and some dip molds in which the deckle simply lies on top of, rather than fits around, the papermaking screen. The effect can be manipulated by relaxing or increasing the pressure with which the deckle is held against the screen.

Question: What if I don't like the imprint of the cover screen (window screen) on the surface of my sheet?

Answer: Anything placed on the surface of a very wet newly formed sheet will imprint or texture it. If you don't like the imprint of the cover screen, don't use it. Instead, use a thin cloth or Pellon (an interfacing used in sewing) which is available at fabric stores. Where directions say to put the cover screen over the new sheet, put cloth or Pellon over it instead. The Pellon can be left on the sheet through all the following steps until the sheet is dry. If drying with heat (by ironing), make sure that what you buy can be ironed.

Question: What if I am getting thin spots in my sheets?

Answer: It is likely less water is draining through the screen at that point because of some obstruction (where less water goes, less fibers go). Pulp has in it unseen matter which (in substandard English) bears the beautiful name of scum. It can't be avoided. It builds up gradually on papermaking screens unless the screens are cleaned regularly. Dipping the screens into clear rinse water after each sheet is excellent prevention. Another problem occurs when little papermaking fibers get stuck in the screen. They will bond and hold to a few neighbors. On succeeding sheet formings, the little neighbors will each grab and hang onto a friend. Soon you will have major blockage in the screen at the fiber's site and a thin spot, or even a hole, in your sheet. The cure is to clean the screen. Use a good kitchen sink spray on it after each papermaking session, or whenever thin spots occur. Normally, holding the screen up to a light will enable the blockage to be seen. By the

way, $250 million paper machines have the same problem. They are fitted with a spray which constantly rinses the screen after the paper web is couched off.

Question: Can I put my handmade paper through a laser printer?

Answer: I have. The printing was very satisfactory. I would not try paper with botanicals or paper with commercial glitter or recycled foil. Though it works, laser printing is not necessarily a good idea. Reports are that handmade paper loses fibers more easily from the surface than do machine-made papers (one factor is likely the difference in pressing pressure),

which can raise havoc with printers. Consequently, without sufficient pressure and sizing to lock fibers firmly to the surface, my answer is, "Yes, but I normally wouldn't."

Question: What if my paper is too thick?

Answer: Put less fiber (pulp) in the deckle. If recycling paper for a single sheet for use in a pour hand mold, put less paper in the blender. For a dip mold, add water (without fiber) to the vat.

Question: Can I scent my paper?

Answer: I have not seen or heard of anything put into pulp prior to sheet forming that will remain as a scent in the dried sheet. Obviously I haven't seen and heard of everything. I'm going to keep looking and listening. But currently, the only route I know to scented paper is scenting dry sheets.

Question: Can I take bad stuff out of my paper?

Answer: Bad stuff, I presume, is spots, zits, dirt specks, or stray bits of botanicals on or near a sheet's surface. Removal has been practiced down through the ages. It is a fine art. The eye delights in detecting immediately the slightest flaw in the smooth distribution of surface fibers. So the answer is, "Yes, but if not done with the utmost care and sensitivity, the eye will know you did it." Much depends on the nature of what is to be removed. Practice, experience, a good magnifying glass, and a longer pin that rests comfortably between your fingers, are necessary. Getting the pin point under an edge of the object and carefully prying it loose, is key. Some might disintegrate, leaving a mess worse than the original flaw. Some materials stain surrounding fibers when removed, making it necessary to remove stained or colored fibers.

Before undertaking removal, analyze the flaw's nature and whether removal damage might be worse than the flaw or might even totally ruin the sheet. If removal has left seriously disrupted surface fibers, sometimes rewetting the sheet with a fine spray and redrying it under pressure will realign fibers and mitigate the flaw. When working with a pin, always work from the flaw's edge toward the center, rather than from the center outward. Less damage is likely. Good luck.

Question: Why doesn't glitter stay in my paper?

Answer: Because it is just resting on the surface rather than actually a part of the sheet. In the pulp in the deckle, glitter tends to float. To tie glitter down, there must be fibers over at least part of each glitter particle. Putting glitter in the blender can help as does vigorously rocking the mold in all directions as the water drains. Try putting very few fibers in the deckle with glitter and literally forming a very thin sheet of fibers and glitter. Then pulp layer the thin sheet onto the surface of your regular sheet. Tying glitter securely into a sheet takes attention. Tying down 100% of the glitter may never happen.

FROM PAPER HISTORY: THREE WORLD-SHAKING MOMENTS
CHAPTER SEVENTEEN

Obviously I'm in trouble for daring to name the three most momentous paper history moments. Hopefully, my mailbox won't melt with the heat of some reactions, and vilification won't spread across the Internet.

However, frequent in-depth and detailed review of paper history through personal conversations with Dard Hunter over a period of five years and during my subsequent curatorship of the Dard Hunter Paper Museum, does endow me with at least somewhat of a qualified background for stepping into this particular lion's mouth.

Further, as shown by my choice for Moment Number Three, I sat adjacent to, and had a minor role in, the making of recent paper history, because if there ever was a place where recent paper history was being made, it was at The Institute of Paper Chemistry. (And that is probably another mail box-filling statement.)

But there is another reason for the three moments I've chosen.

This book would not be complete without paper history. But when I see "History of Paper" in an index, and the book has allotted two or three pages to it, I feel faint. What mighty and omniscient mind has seized centuries of bark-peeling, endless years of vat-side movement, acres of rice fields, wars, beating and pounding, rag picking, tree cutting and planting, pouring of molten matter into forms at foundries, laboratory work, papermaking screen development from woven grasses to multi-weave synthetic strands, a wedding between U2 aircraft and filter paper, and the current trouble of PCBs and the EPA, and jammed it all into two pages—with margins.

The question is unfair. There have to be two-page histories of paper. But what an immense deletion of material—facts, drama, pathos, defeat, victory, disappointment, and almost continual world shaking.

So let this book maintain an honest perspective. The history it presents on a few pages is definitely no paper's history. It is simply choosing and briefly addressing three magnificent, amazing, world-shaking paper history moments.

Moment One

The invention of paper. When was it and who was the inventor? We don't really know. Was it the prestigious Chinese courtier Ts'ai Lun, operating in the rare air of the Chinese Imperial Court, or some unknown peasant operating in some offbeat Chinese backwash?

What we do know is the date paper's invention was first recorded. That date is 105 A.D. in the official Chinese chronicles.

The chronicle language refers to "Ts'ai Lun's paper," which has led to his being identified in subsequent literature as the inventor.

That is somewhat logical. Ts'ai Lun was an official who bought supplies for the Court. He was, in a way, a buyer for a very big operation. Among things he likely shopped for were writing materials on which to keep, among other things, the official chronicles.

Other writings confirm there was at the time a serious ongoing search for writing materials better than bamboo, silk, tortoise bones, etc. Who would be more likely to become aware of a better writing material than Ts'ai Lun?

And after having heard about it, tried it, found it great, and introduced it into the purchasing lists of the Imperial Court, who would be more likely to be identified with it than Ts'ai Lun?

Another scenario favorable to Ts'ai Lun is as follows. His job of providing good things for the Court might well have led him personally, or by supervision of others, into concerted research for better writing materials. Such research might have produced paper, justifying his being called paper's inventor.

But there are anti-Ts'ai Lun facts. Archeological digs have provided evidence from which can be deduced that paper existed centuries before Ts'ai Lun was ever heard of. But this is deduction, not proven fact. Paper has been found in the presence of materials dating much earlier than Ts'ai Lun. But this leaves open the possibility that a collection of older artifacts got somehow buried with some paper at a date after Ts'ai Lun.

Further muddying the true invention date is the question of what the first paper was called by the Chinese, and the problem of doing research in the old Chinese language (try reading Old English). There being no word for something that doesn't exist, the Chinese had to give paper a name upon its invention. Was it a word, or adaptation of a word, that previously existed? How long was it before a single name, from among possibly several names used at first, was agreed upon?

This lingual maze and its ramifications are treated most interestingly and lucidly by Ts'un Tsien in his book, *Written on Bamboo and Silk* (see Bibliography). My awareness of all this came during a visit by Dr. Tsien to the Dard Hunter Paper Museum while I was curator.

Everything considered, paper's invention remains an interesting and fascinating moment, certainly world shaking, but when was it? The only statement I will make is that paper certainly was in existence in the year 105 A.D. because it was recorded as an invention in that year.

Nicholas-Louis Robert, inventor of the papermaking machine. (Courtesy of the Robert C. Williams American Museum of Papermaking, featuring the Dard Hunter Collection.)

Moment Two

The invention of the paper machine. Another magnificent, amazing, world-shaking moment occurred in France in 1798. It was brought about by an ex-soldier who took work in a paper mill. He was Nicholas-Louis Robert and he invented the paper machine.

That moment's magnificence is that it was another great triumph of the human mind. It moved a process from single sheet making, which had been unchanged by other minds for 1,600 years, to a process of continual web-making. The moment changed paper forming-to-drying from a three-man process to a no-man process. It made obsolete a whole class of highly skilled craftsmen who made hand molds, wiping out another apprenticeship field.

The moment was amazing also for what caused it to happen. Robert, the inventor, said he invented the machine because he couldn't stand the papermakers' (vat men, couchers, laymen) constant bickering, fighting, and arguing. It was an amazing moment in which man's irascibility turned back on him.

The moment was world shaking in that it made possible the production of all the paper needed for rapid advancement of information distribution, knowledge, commerce, and science. This would never have been possible had paper continued to be made one sheet at a time. There was already a law in England limiting the size of newspaper sheets. Today, paper machines can make paper a mile a minute.

Ironically, neither Robert nor the Fourdrinier Brothers of England who financed its development into commercial feasibility, made any money from it. Everyone else did and continues to today. Robert died a poorly paid school teacher. The Fourdrinier Brothers went bankrupt.

Moment Three

IPC 1478 Filter Paper. With misgivings, we move past the momentous date of circa 1865 which saw freedom from limitation of rags gained by Western papermakers and entry into the practically unlimited world of wood as a fiber source. This led to another amazing moment 100 years later—production of the world's first test tube tree (clone) at The Institute of Paper Chemistry on November 1, 1968. But my selection for the third moment is something that occurred in the decades after World War II and related to the dropping of two atomic bombs.

The world's entry into the atomic weapons age engendered a race for guaranteed survival by maintenance of atomic weapon supremacy. Further weapons development required testing atomic devices. In the postwar era, this meant exploding devices in the atmosphere.

Somewhere along the line, simple awareness of deposition of radioactive materials in the atmosphere and the descending of the particles to earth, became an acute worry.

This led to establishment of an appropriate U.S. governmental group to assay the situation of atmospheric radioactive debris, learn something of its dynamics, and determine the degree of hazard to humanity. Sufficient funding was provided and the work was classified.

Some of the funding went to research at The Institute of Paper Chemistry. The result was a revolutionary filter paper that was sufficiently "loose" to let air pass through at 60 miles an hour, yet "tight" enough to filter from the air, at near 100% efficiency, particles of an angstrom in diameter. The two qualities are diametrically opposed. The unusual paper was made in the Institute's pulp laboratory by hand until a machine could be suitably modified.

The moment at which there was finally a piece of paper that passed laboratory tests, and the work could validly be declared successful, was a magnificent, amazing, world-shaking moment in paper history.

IPC 1478 filter paper, as it was called, was subsequently linked with several of the first U2 aircraft ("spy" plane) built. The aircraft were modified to carry the filter paper. In an extended program of flights from a variety of bases internationally, the filter paper, transported by the speed and altitude capabilities of the aircraft, sampled the entire atmosphere of the earth, according to a government report. The third element of the effort, a mathematical formula, made possible a meaningful extrapolation from what the paper collected.

The undertaking identified sites of radioactive concentrations, the rate at which debris ascended, the altitude reached, characteristics of the horizontal drift, and locale and rate of descent. Any new explosions were detected and characterized.

On the basis of data delivered by the paper, it was determined that continued atmospheric testing constituted a biological hazard to humanity. It was discontinued.

By this program, paper touched every human, animal, and individual plant on the face of the earth directly.

That should qualify for magnificent, amazing, and world shaking.

After being declassified, the work was announced at the next Annual Executives Conference of The Institute of Paper Chemistry. I had the pleasure of breaking the story to the media.

A moment also outstanding occurs when one makes paper and thereby joins an activity that has been going on, unbroken, for almost (or possibly more than) 2,000 years.

THE
PAPERMAKER'S TEAR
CHAPTER EIGHTEEN

In forensics, the ability to tell whether a sheet of paper is handmade or machine-made, can sometimes be frighteningly important. There are quite a few people who claim they can tell without fail, but most of the time this is more ego than truth.

What I learned during my years at The Institute of Paper Chemistry and my curatorship of the Dard Hunter Paper Museum has led me to believe that one of the few ways—maybe the only way—to tell is the "papermaker's tear."

Time has dimmed my memory of the precise moment I became aware of this phenomenon. It might have been one of those rare mo-ments with Dard Hunter when the mood was mellow and the words free and easy. Or it might have been one of his comments while examining a sheet held to the light. Almost surely it was in the Dard Hunter Paper Museum.

But whether it came during straight pedantic exposition or a bit of verbal enjoyment in a relaxed moment of paper-based camaraderie, the informa-tion struck me with durable impact. I will never for-get it. That first view of the phenomenon left me with an impression that what I was seeing was a relation-ship made up of a bit of regret, yet was precious and personal, certainly intimate, between a papermaker and his sheet.

A papermaker's tear is the falling of a drop of water, probably always from a lifted deckle, onto the pristine surface of a newly-formed sheet. The drop's impact displaces numerous of the weakly bonded fibers. This makes the sheet thinner where the fibers were. After drying, the sheet is held up to the light. Quite visible is a tell-tale spot of brightness in an otherwise uni-form, darker level of light transmitted through the sheet.

It can look something like a moon crater. The physics are similar: a meteor crashes into the moon's surface and dis-places moon matter—a water drop crashes into the sheet's surface and dis-places fibers.

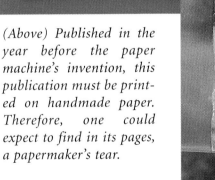

(Above) Published in the year before the paper machine's invention, this publication must be print-ed on handmade paper. Therefore, one could expect to find in its pages, a papermaker's tear.

Sure enough. On page 151, in the upper right hand quadrant, there it glows—the still visible effect of a drop of water that fell over two centuries ago.

About the Author

Arnold Grummer loves making paper and has spent most of his life engaged in this fascinating process. He is a former editor and faculty member of the Institute of Paper Chemistry and served as the curator of the Dard Hunter Paper Museum. In addition to authoring two best-selling papermaking books and three videos on the subject, Arnold has spoken and lectured throughout the country and regularly demonstrates paper-making for Greg Markim, Inc., a leading papermaking supply company.

Bibliography

Barrett, Timothy, *Japanese Papermaking,* Weatherhill, New York and Tokyo, 1983

Bell, Lilian, *Plant Fibers for Papermaking,* Liliaceae Press, McMinnville, OR, 1988

Grummer, Arnold, *Paper by Kids,* Dillon Press, Minneapolis, 1980 (now the property of Greg Markim, Inc., Milwaukee)

Grummer, Arnold, *Tin Can Papermaking,* Greg Markim, Inc., Milwaukee, 1992

Heller, Jules, *Papermaking,* Watson-Guptill Publications, New York, 1978

Hunter, Dard, *Papermaking: The History and Technique of an Ancient Craft,* Dover Publications, New York (Paperback), 1978

Koretsky, Elaine, *Color for the Hand Papermaker,* Carriage House Press, Brookline, MA, 1983

Mason, John, *Papermaking as an Artistic Craft,* Faber and Faber Ltd., London, 1959

Richardson, M., *Plant Papers,* Berrington Press, Hereford, 1986

Saddington, Marianne, *Making Your Own Paper,* Storey Commuinications, Inc., Pownel, VT, 1992

Studley, Vance, *The Art and Craft of Handmade Paper,* Dover Publications, NY 1977

Toale, Bernard, *The Art of Papermaking,* Davis Publications, Worcester, MA, 1983

Tsien, Tsuen-Hsuin, *Written on Bamboo and Silk,* University of Chicago Press, Chicago, 1962

Appendix

Buying Information

The source for kits and individual components associated with the pour hand mold is my hand papermaking craft company, Greg Markim, Inc. The company offers all items mentioned in the basic hand papermaking steps, plus accessories such as double deckles, metallic glitters, flower packets, etc. and a set of three videos showing art and decorative techniques. The videos were very favorably reviewed in the *Library Journal* of September 1, 1997. Currently, Greg Markim, Inc. is the sole source of pour hand mold kits. But some of the other sources listed might be distributors of Greg Markim, Inc. products, videos, books, and kits. Each source has an extensive line of new pulps, cotton linters, etc. Several also offer a wide range of prepared dyes, sizings, and other products. All offer dip hand molds and kits. No kits include blenders, vats, trays, or irons.

Greg Markim, Inc.
P.O. Box 13245
Milwaukee, WI 53213
Phone (414) 453-1480
Fax (414) 453-1495
Orders (800) 453-1485
Website:
www.arnoldgrummer.com
Arnold Grummer's Paper
Making Supplies and
Casting Molds

Twinrocker
100 East Third St.
P.O. Box 413
Brookston, IN 47923
Phone (800) 757-TWIN
Website:
   www.twinrocker.com
Papermaking supplies

Carriage House Paper
79 Guernsey St.
Brooklyn, NY 11222
Phone & Fax:
   (718) 599-7857
Orders (800) 669-8781
Technical assistance
   (617) 232-1636
Papermaking supplies

Gold's Artworks, Inc.
2100 N. Pine St.
Lumberton, NC 28358
Phone (919) 739-9605
Outside North Carolina
   (800) 356-2306
Papermaking supplies

Paper Museums

Robert C. Williams American Museum of Papermaking
500 10th St. NW, Atlanta, GA 30318
Phone (404) 894-7840
The Dard Hunter Paper Museum of which I am a former curator is now part of the Robert C. Williams American Museum of Papermaking. However, the Dard Hunter materials constitute what is most likely the world's most comprehensive assemblage of international materials, according to Henk Voorn, former President of the International Paper Historians. The American Museum of Papermaking is in turn part of the Institute of Paper Science and Technology, the successor organization to the former Institute of Paper Chemistry. The Institute and the museum are now located in Atlanta, Georgia.

Crane & Co., Inc.
30 South St., Dalton, MA 01226
Open hours: 2 to 5 p.m.
June 1 through mid-October.
Crane & Company, Inc. has a long history in American papermaking, including currency manufacture. A small company museum is maintained.

Index